# FLYING SCOTSMAN

# FLYING SCOTSMAN

**David McIntosh**

Ian Allan
PUBLISHING

First published 2010

ISBN 978 0 7110 3533 1

© David McIntosh 2010

Published by Ian Allan Publishing

an imprint of Ian Allan Publishing Ltd, Hersham, Surrey, KT12 4RG

Printed in England by Ian Allan Printing Ltd, Hersham, Surrey, KT12 4RG

Code: 1011/C3

Distributed in the United States of America and Canada by BookMasters Distribution Services

Visit the Ian Allan Publishing website at www.ianallanpublishing.com

*Front cover:* No 4472, whilst paired with No 4498's tender, heads the southbound 'Cumbrian Mountain Pullman' out of Rise Hill Tunnel on 26 June 1983. *J. H. Cooper-Smith*

*Back cover:* During its 1988/9 tour of Australia, No 4472 is seen near Dry Creek, South Australia. *R. Currie*

*Half title page:* No 4472 hauls a Leeds-Birmingham empty stock train which includes saloon No GE 1 past Clay Cross on 27 December 1985. *Paul Stratford*

*Title page:* On 1 May 1987 No 4472 brings the stock for the first of a series of 'Cromwell Pullman' charters into Leicester station prior to departure for Stratford-upon-Avon. *Paul A. Biggs*

# Contents

The locomotive No 4472 (for that has been her number for 72 out of her 87 years' existence) is a famous icon recognised the world over because of her name, *Flying Scotsman*, and thus her association, and frequent confusion with, the famous train of the same name, and for the world records that she holds. First, in 1928 she hauled the inaugural northbound non-stop 'Flying Scotsman' train over the world-record 392.9 miles from King's Cross to Edinburgh. Although during the 1948 diversions following the summer flood damage to the regular route, eight different 'A4' 'Pacifics' extended this record to 408.6 miles, it was No 4472 herself who reclaimed the record on 8 August 1989 with a never again to be challenged run of no less than 422 miles while visiting Australia. In 1934 she was the very first steam locomotive to achieve a fully authenticated speed of 100mph. Also during the course of her visit to Australia in 1988-89, she became the first steam locomotive to complete a circumnavigation of the globe, travelling out via Suez and returning via Panama.

Although only the third British steam locomotive to run main-line trips in North America, the 1969-73 visit of No 4472 established a

*Flying Scotsman* was invited to Australia as part of that country's bicentennial celebrations. On 24 July 1989 No 4472 is losing the battle against Nos T362 and X45 on a down broad gauge empty ballast train as the two trains pull away from Wallan and climb the grade towards Heathcote junction on the Melbourne-Albury line. *Graham Withers*

much higher profile than that of her two predecessors, largely because of the worldwide nature of the modern media. The financial failure of the visit precipitated the first of several high-profile financial problems that appear to have dogged the locomotive during the last 37 years. It is difficult to escape the conclusion that the glamour and prestige associated with No 4472 has sometimes so affected the judgement of her owners that unwise ventures and expenditure have put the future of the locomotive at serious risk. Having become public property between 1948 and 1963, in 2004 No 4472 became a publicly owned treasure once again, and hopefully, with the completion of her latest and somewhat protracted overhaul due in 2011, she will again grace the metals of the UK rail network and be admired by all who see her as she approaches her centenary.

This book attempts to tell the story of this famous locomotive, including both the high and some very low points as accurately and fairly as possible. Now under her sixth and hopefully most secure ownership, I hope her creator Sir Nigel Gresley would regard this work as a fitting tribute to one of his most iconic creations, and hope that No 4472 will continue to give as much pleasure to future generations as she has to those who have known and loved this fine example of one of man's most amazing creations, the steam locomotive!

## Acknowledgements

Much of the material in this volume has come from the personal reminiscences of those responsible for the upkeep of No 4472 both before and after 1963. Particular thanks are due to George Hinchcliffe and Roland Kennington who gave freely of their time and memories, to colleagues in the Gresley Society for references, articles and photographs from their archives and their Journal *The Gresley Observer*, to the many photographers who searched their files to seek out interesting material, particularly Peter Groom and David Percival, and to David Postle and my friends at the Kidderminster Railway Museum for photographs, access to reference materials, advice and support. The opinions expressed are entirely my own and any errors are of course my responsibility alone.

On 16 September 1911, on reaching the age of 60, H. A. Ivatt retired after 15 years of distinguished service as the Locomotive Engineer of the Great Northern Railway. He was succeeded from 1 October by the 35-year-old Herbert Nigel Gresley, who had been the railway's Carriage & Wagon Superintendent since 1905. Despite his relative youth, Gresley had already established himself as an innovative rolling stock engineer with several patents granted for new concepts, prominent among which was one for the articulation of carriages, a principle still used today in many parts of the world, most notably for the TGV and Eurostar train fleets. Gresley was Ivatt's recommended successor to the GNR Board, having for several years past become regarded as his chief assistant, and his initial salary was a significantly increased £1,800 per annum. A rival candidate with significantly more experience in locomotive matters was Francis Wintour, the Works Manager at Doncaster. Despite the rebuff to any personal ambitions of his own, Wintour became a loyal and close colleague, soon joined by Oliver Bulleid as Gresley's

personal assistant, and Edward Thompson as C&W Superintendent.

Ivatt had left behind an excellent inheritance for Gresley, a complete series of standardised locomotives more than adequate for the tasks imposed upon them, with the sole exception of a large mixed-traffic locomotive able to work the increasingly important fast freight trains. It has often been claimed that Gresley's first priority on assuming the Locomotive Engineer's position was to produce a design of express passenger locomotive of greater size and power than the Ivatt large-boilered wide-firebox 'Atlantic'. A study of the GNR Board minutes and the minutes of the Locomotive Committee reveals to the contrary that one of Gresley's first non-routine reports, as early as 23 January 1912, was to highlight the amount of goods train mileage being hauled by passenger engines and the urgent need for more powerful goods engines capable of hauling heavier trains at speeds of 30 to 40mph. There were currently 393 passenger locomotives as against only 405 0-6-0 goods engines, while the percentage of goods to passenger mileage was increasing. This was followed in August by the issue of revised Loading of Goods Trains, which increased tonnage by 5.6% and led to a reduction in goods train miles of 1.45%, albeit at increased coal consumption per mile.

The priority was therefore to build a larger stud of heavy goods locomotives, particularly for the heavy flow of coal traffic from South Yorkshire and Nottinghamshire to London. These were being worked principally by the 55 Ivatt 'Long Tom' 'K1' and 'K2' 0-8-0s dating from between 1901 and 1909. Also in August 1912 emerged Gresley's first design, a very advanced mixed-traffic 'Mogul', the 'H2' 2-6-0 (later 'K1' class). No 1630 was also the first GNR locomotive to be equipped with Walschaerts valve gear, apart from four four-cylinder 'Atlantics' and six steam rail-motors. This was soon followed in December 1913 by Gresley's second design, the 'O1' class of large two-cylinder 2-8-0s, also provided with Walschaerts valve gear driving 10-inch piston valves.

Next to emerge in 1913 was the first Gresley tank engine design, the 'J23' (later 'J50' and 'J51'), an 0-6-0T particularly well adapted for operation on the heavy grades of the West Riding where good adhesion was an essential factor. In 1914 came the enlarged 'H3' 2-6-0 (later 'K2'). Although plans for a three-cylinder 2-8-0 mineral engine had been drawn up in 1916, the demand for munitions took priority for both workshop capacity and materials, and there was therefore a gap of almost four years before the next design emerged, the 'O2' 2-8-0. In October 1916 Gresley had been granted the patent rights for a conjugate valve gear for three-cylinder locomotives, employing rocking shafts or motion levers. The 'O2' that appeared in May 1918 was Gresley's first three-cylinder locomotive and it embodied the alternative form of his conjugate valve gear, with rocking shafts to operate the middle valve. Another feature to become a Gresley standard was to have the drive from all cylinders connected to the same axle. Next, in December 1918, the first outline drawings emerged of a much enlarged three-cylinder 2-6-0, which became the 'H4' (later 'K3'), the first example of which, No 1000, appeared in March 1920. Gresley had now decided to use 2-to-1 levers ahead of the cylinders instead of a rocking shaft behind them, another future Gresley standard feature. In December 1920 the second design of Gresley tank engine emerged, the 'N2' 0-6-2T. These were an enlarged version of the Ivatt 'N1' class with piston valves and superheaters, which became the standard London area commuter service locomotive for the next 40 years. Now, some ten years after he had taken control of GNR locomotive matters, the scene was set for Gresley's eighth locomotive design.

On 10 January 1921 the GNR ordered two 'Pacific'-type locomotives to a new design, and on 30 March 1922 the first of Gresley's 'A1' 'Pacifics', No 1470 *Great Northern*, emerged from Doncaster Works. No 1470 was only the second GNR locomotive to be given the prestige of a name, and this was probably a high-profile way of acknowledging the company's desire to commemorate the 73 years of the GNR before its pending absorption into the new LNER on 1 January 1923. This new design of locomotive incorporated all three of the distinctive design principles with which Gresley was to become associated throughout his career. The first was the use of three-cylinder propulsion with the operation of the inside valves derived from the valve gear of the outside cylinders. Initially Gresley had rebuilt an Ivatt 'Atlantic' in 1915 with four cylinders and outside Walschaerts valve gear operating the inside piston valves by means of rocking shafts, and in 1916 his attention had been drawn to the publication in *Engineering* of detailed drawings of a Pennsylvania Railroad 'K4s' 'Pacific' locomotive. Gresley is reported to have been very impressed by the proportions of the

'K4s'. The GNR structure gauge could not accommodate the large outside cylinders of the two-cylinder 'K4s' and the three-cylinder arrangement had already been successfully applied in 1918 to the 'O2' version of his 2-8-0 and, in 1920, to the enlarged 2-6-0, which became the 'K3'. Gresley settled on the three-cylinder arrangement as offering the advantages of a more even turning moment leading to less wear and tear to a locomotive's motion and a significant reduction in the hammer

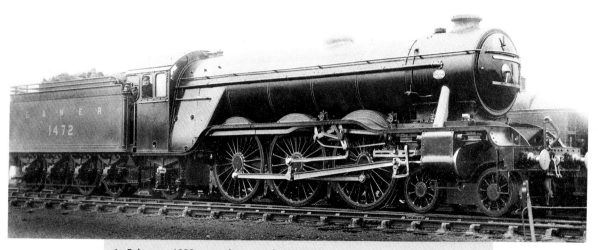

In February 1923 recently ex-works LNER No 1472 is pictured on King's Cross shed in original condition, unnamed, GNR structure gauge, no brass beading on the splashers and blank cabsides. *Ian Allan Library*

blow experienced in two-cylinder designs, offering less wear on the track and structures and the possibility of lighter valve gear and reciprocating parts. The other principles were that all three cylinders should drive the same axle, and that this should not be the leading coupled axle.

*Great Northern* was, of course, not Britain's first 'Pacific', that honour belonging to Churchward's *The Great Bear* of 1908 for the Great Western Railway. But whereas the GWR 'Pacific' could hardly be regarded as a successful design (Collett is reported to have remarked on seeing the first pictures of No 1470, 'Why did Mr Gresley want to build his own "Pacific" – we could have let him have ours') and remained the sole representative of its class, Gresley had produced a design that, with later modifications, was to extend to a total of 114 engines. He incorporated all that he considered best in contemporary British and US practice – large boiler with wide firebox, three cylinders, and high running plate – all contributing to a well-proportioned 'Pacific'. The original 'A1' 'Pacific' had a front end designed on lines that were then more

or less traditional in Great Britain. The valve motion was arranged with a maximum travel of 4⅚ inches at 75% cut-off; this was the biggest cut-off at which the engines could be worked. This limitation was due to the fact that the previous 'K3' 2-6-0s had been found to damage the covers of their inside cylinder valve chests by overrunning of the valve spindle when coasting at their full 75% cut-off with their regulators shut. With such a valve setting the 'A1s' had to be worked at long cut-offs, often up to 45 or 50% with the fastest and heaviest trains, and with partially closed regulators. Their well-designed boilers and sharp blast resulting from such methods of working always guaranteed plenty of steam, but at a cost of an average coal consumption on all duties, heavy and light, as high as 50lb per mile. However, Gresley's objective for the class was the ability to haul 600-ton trains to the schedules of the day, with average speeds of around 50mph, and this they proved well capable of doing.

The second Gresley 'A1' 'Pacific', No 1471, emerged in July 1922. Initially unnamed, this

In the summer of 1923 the driver is applying sand as No 1472 accelerates her express for the North past Belle Isle signal box on leaving King's Cross. The locomotive is still in original condition. *Ian Allan Library*

This official March 1924 Doncaster Works photo shows the now LNER No 4472 *Flying Scotsman* as prepared for the British Empire Exhibition with the LNER coat of arms on the cabside, brass beading on the splashers, burnished wheel rims, motion and fittings, and original short nameplate. To preserve the exhibition finish the locomotive was moved south enveloped in a protective sheet. *Ian Allan Library*

locomotive was subsequently named after the last Chairman of the GNR, Sir Frederick Banbury. The GNR already had enough confidence in the design to place an order, also in July 1922, for a further ten 'Pacifics', and Doncaster Works responded so rapidly that the third locomotive,

No 1472, was delivered in February 1923, just after the January absorption of the GNR into the new LNER. Despite this the locomotive was delivered with a GNR number, but lettered on the tender 'L&NER'. Only in early 1924, when being prepared for her exhibition at Wembley, did she acquire the complete LNER livery and the number 4472, together with the name *Flying Scotsman*.

Of the first 12 'A1' 'Pacifics' in service by September 1923, seven were allocated to Doncaster shed, including Nos 1470, 1471 and 1472, three to Grantham, and only two to King's Cross. This very much reflected the traditional GNR predominance of Doncaster shed (coded Shed 1) in the fastest and heaviest East Coast workings. In part this was caused by the principal West Riding trains being among the heaviest and the weight restrictions over the Calder Viaduct at Wakefield, which, until July 1930, forced locomotive changes at Doncaster for 'Pacific'-hauled trains. The decline in the role of Doncaster began to escalate with the commencement of the Newcastle non-stop workings in 1927, although the total lack of involvement of this shed in the Locomotive Exchange workings in 1925 proved a foretaste of the future and the ultimate decline in the role of Doncaster Carr Loco in the principal East Coast workings. Despite this, the tradition still survived in part as late as 1938, as Doncaster was the home of

the famous No 4468 *Mallard* for the first five years of her service.

## The 1923 Exchange Trials with the ex-NER Raven 'Pacific'

In March 1922 Darlington Works had been authorised to build two 'Pacific' locomotives to a new design by the NER Locomotive Superintendent, Sir Vincent Raven. These were in effect a stretched version of his highly successful 'Z' (later 'C7') class three-cylinder 'Atlantic' type, which had monopolised East Coast workings between York and Edinburgh since 1911. The design proved successful enough for a further three to be authorised just after the Grouping, on 22 February 1923, in what appears to be a rather desperate anticipation by Darlington of the formal appointment one day later of Nigel Gresley as the Chief Mechanical Engineer of the new LNER. In fact, before these three engines were constructed in March 1924 Gresley authorised some minor changes in the design to incorporate the Cartazzi axle-boxes and outside rear-end framing of the type used in his 'A1' class. With two of the new Raven 'Pacifics' and seven 'A1s' available by the end of May 1923, it was decided to conduct some comparative trials between the two new 'Pacific' designs. Between 25 June and 4 July 1923 Nos 4472 (the still unnamed 'A1') and 2400 (of the new 'A2' class, also as yet unnamed) each ran three double trips in ordinary service between Doncaster and King's Cross, with the addition of the ex-NER Dynamometer Car as the leading vehicle. The results of the tests revealed very little difference between the two types, with the 'A2' having the edge in steam production and the 'A1' being marginally more economical on coal per drawbar horsepower hour. The fate of the 'A2s' was inevitably sealed in October 1923 when a further 20 'A1s' were ordered from Doncaster and a further 20 at the same time from the North British Locomotive Co.

## The British Empire Exhibition at Wembley

The LNER was rightly proud of its new 'Pacifics', and in 1924-25 arranged for the third engine, and first post-Grouping example, by now numbered No 4472 and named *Flying Scotsman*, to appear as an exhibit in the Palace of Engineering at the British Empire Exhibition at Wembley. For this high-profile event No 4472 was returned to Doncaster at the end of December 1923 and, during a nine-week stay, was given a special exhibition finish with the LNER coat of arms on a panel on the cabside, burnished tyres, polished brass splasher beading and all brightwork highly polished. No 4472 actually had two separate spells at Wembley in the summers of both 1924 and 1925. On the second visit there was less space available and a shorter six-wheel tender, No 5378, was borrowed from a 'K3', suitably repainted to match the locomotive.

No 4472 returned to normal main-line service in November 1925 and settled down to the regular work of a Doncaster-based 'Pacific', hauling services mainly between Doncaster and London. One change in her appearance, implemented in March 1928, was the reversion to cab-side numbers. The practice since 1923 had been for the locomotive number to be carried on the tender, beneath the LNER branding. Since during works visits tenders tended to be exchanged between locomotives, this practice could and did occasionally cause problems, so was abandoned in 1928; previous practice was reverted to, with the locomotive number being displayed on the cab side, the tender only carrying the branding 'LNER'.

On 10 October 1925 No 4472 is almost at the end of the second period of display at the British Empire Exhibition at Wembley, now for space reasons coupled to a shorter tender, No 5378, borrowed from a K3 2-6-0. *Ken Nunn collection*

## The 1925 Locomotive Exchanges

Next to No 4472 at Wembley in 1924 was the newly completed GWR 4-6-0 No 4073 *Caerphilly Castle*. Noticeably smaller and of an earlier, Edwardian, appearance, the 'Castle' carried a prominent notice proclaiming it to be the most powerful locomotive in the British Isles. As the 'Castle' was of modest size in comparison with the 'A1', it became a talking point.

The matter was to be settled by trial when, in April and May 1925, exchanges were arranged under which an LNER 'Pacific' was to run on the Great Western from Paddington to Plymouth in comparative tests with a native 'Castle', while a 'Pacific' and a 'Castle' would be similarly pitted against one another on the LNER between King's Cross, Grantham and Doncaster. Surprisingly,

In the summer of 1926 No 4472 is now running in normal express service in ex-Wembley condition but still with short-travel valves and with her original tender restored after the exhibition. Still shedded at Doncaster, No 4472 is seen here passing Wood Green with a heavy down express. *Ian Allan Library*

Gresley was not apparently consulted before the trials were instituted, which were said to have been the result of a social conversation between Sir Felix Pole, the GWR General Manager, and, depending on the source, either LNER Chairman Ralph Wedgwood or Alex Wilson, the LNER's Southern Area Divisional General Manager. Gresley had agreed with his opposite number Collett of the GWR that the results would not be publicised until both had had the opportunity to analyse them properly. Paddington, however, had other ideas, and made much of the claimed 'victory' of its locomotives. Indeed, the 'Castles', with Churchward's valve setting and 225psi pressure, had proved that they could make better times than the 180psi Gresley engines and on lower fuel consumption, whether with Welsh or Yorkshire coal.

O. S. Nock relates the story that Gresley visited Paddington early in the week of the trials with the 'Cornish Riviera Express' to meet No 4474 (then unnamed but later *Victor Wild*) and her crew on arrival. The LNER footplate representative was E. D. Trask, later to become Locomotive Running Superintendent for the Southern Area of the LNER. Answering a query to Trask as to how they were doing, Trask is reported to have replied, 'All right, but not as well as the GW.' Gresley is supposed to have responded, 'Oh, but you must,' to which Trask replied, 'I don't see how we can. They've got a better valve gear than ours.' Gresley apparently retorted, 'Mr Wintour [Locomotive Works Manager at Doncaster] is getting out a modified form of ours,' to which Trask replied, 'Well, that won't be much good to us this week!'

On the LNER the tests were conducted between London and Grantham or Doncaster, the locomotives involved being GWR No 4079 *Pendennis Castle* and No 4475 *Flying Fox*. On her very first down trip No 4475 failed with a hot box and had to be replaced by No 2545 *Diamond Jubilee*. The result was not all bad for the LNER, as Gresley was forced to reconsider elements of his 'Pacific' design, particularly the poor valve events given by the short-travel valve gear, so that ultimately the losers came to benefit most from the experience.

**B**ert Spencer, Gresley's chief technical assistant and the man responsible for the design of the characteristic 'Gresley' side-window cab, had already tried in 1924 to persuade his boss to introduce long-lap, long-travel valve gear, but without success. Not afraid of a little industrial espionage, the LNER had examined the valve gear arrangements of No 4079 *Pendennis Castle* at Doncaster shed before the trials in April 1925, and in June of the same year No 4082 *Windsor Castle* was similarly examined while stabled in Faverdale Wagon Works prior to exhibition at the Stockton & Darlington Railway centenary celebrations. The CME's reluctance to alter a design still comparatively new, and which, although with some concerns regarding fuel consumption, was master of the tasks it was being set, was understandable. Eventually in 1926 Spencer was allowed to fit his own design of valve gear, first to 'A1' No 4477 *Gay Crusader*, with a 1½-inch instead of 1¼-inch lap, then to 'A1' No 2555 *Centenary*, which also had its maximum valve travel increased to 5¾ inches. New narrow-ringed piston valves were also fitted, and the locomotive was tested on the road, where it showed remarkable fuel economy, average fuel consumption falling to 38lb per mile from the original 50lb. After Gresley took the opportunity to observe this more economical working personally from the footplate, he ordered all of the class to be so altered. No 4472 received the long-travel valve modification during a General Overhaul at Doncaster in February/March 1928. Gresley had also been convinced that the higher boiler pressure of the GWR engines had something to do with their economy, so in 1927 higher-pressure 220psi boilers, which also had a much larger superheater, were fitted to Nos 4480 *Enterprise* and 2544 *Lemberg*. The locomotives were an instant success and extremely powerful, so much so that future 'A3s' (for this was the prototype) were built with smaller cylinders of 19 inches by 26 inches. From August 1928 to February 1935 Doncaster turned out 27 new 'A3s', and all but the first of the 'A1s' were rebuilt to conform. All valve gear modifications were completed by 1931, but the higher-pressure boiler conversions took much longer, only being completed well after the

war years. The typical LNER sense of economy dictated that new boilers would only be constructed when the useful life of the original boilers had expired. Thus No 4472 had to wait until 1947 before finally receiving the higher-pressure boiler and being rebuilt to full 'A3' specification.

## The non-stop 'Flying Scotsman'

The economy of the new engines now facilitated a change in train working that saw, in the Summer timetable of 1928, the principal daytime Anglo-Scottish express, the 'Flying Scotsman', altered to commence the longest non-stop schedule in railway history, the 392-mile journey from King's Cross to Edinburgh. In part this was a response to the initiative of the LMS, which had with the Winter 1927/28 timetable begun to run the newly named 'Royal Scot' non-stop over the 299 miles between Euston and Carlisle. The winter portion of the new 'Royal Scot' included a six-coach portion with its own dining and kitchen car for Edinburgh, so this was in direct competition with the LNER service from King's Cross. The old 'gentleman's agreement'

On 1 May 1928 No 4472 heads the inaugural northbound non-stop 'Flying Scotsman' away from King's Cross. Her number has now been transferred to the cabside, and she has a corridor tender, long-travel valves, short chimney, reduced-height boiler mountings and front buffer beam corners cut away. *J. H. L. Adams collection, KRM 015653*

on minimum times to Edinburgh still applied, but the publicity value of the 'non-stop' claim could not be ignored. It had been felt that the limit of the powers of a single engine crew had been reached in the Newcastle non-stop running of the summer service of 1927, and that it was undesirable on grounds of safety to carry two crews on one engine, so the idea of the corridor tender was conceived.

On 30 September 1927 an order had been placed with Doncaster for ten new 'A3'-type 'Pacifics', which emerged as Nos 2743-2752. An associated tender order, No 50, was included. These were to emerge as tenders Nos 5323-5332, with an amended design incorporating a side corridor to enable the exchange of crews on the run and facilitate the safe operation of the new non-stop service planned for the Summer 1928 timetable. Originally it had been planned for both the daytime 'Flying Scotsman' and the overnight 'Night Scotsman' services to be run non-stop, and this is probably why as many as ten corridor tenders were constructed. However, the proposed non-stop operation of the 'Night Scotsman' was never implemented. In an exercise to determine the optimum dimensions of the side corridor, Gresley apparently undertook trials with his family at home utilising dining chairs to confirm the required minimum dimensions of the corridor. In addition to

In the summer of 1929 No 4472 heads the 13-carriage down 'Flying Scotsman' past Greenwood.
*Ian Allan Library*

In 1931 No 4472 heads the up 'Flying Scotsman' south of Grantham. *Gresley Society collection*

On 22 July 1932 No 4472 nears journey's end with the down 'Flying Scotsman' at Craigentinny. *Pamlin Prints/Gresley Society collection*

the side-corridor feature, the tender was redesigned to carry an extra ton of coal. Having received new long-travel valves, cut-down cab and boiler mountings to fit the less generous loading gauge north of York during a visit to Doncaster Works in February and March 1928, No 4472 was selected, with Nos 4476 and 2547, to be one of the three Southern Area locomotives nominated for use on the new service. Accordingly she acquired brand-new corridor tender No 5323 before leaving Doncaster Works and was reallocated to King's Cross shed as from 11 April 1928.

Thus at 10.00am on 1 May 1928 the longest non-stop working in the world ever to be worked by a locomotive of any kind was inaugurated by Driver Pebworth with No 4472 *Flying Scotsman* from King's Cross, and No 2580 *Shotover* from Edinburgh Waverley. On the down run some anxious moments were caused north of Newcastle when a tender axlebox showed signs of overheating, but the journey was still completed 12 minutes early! No 4472 was well enough to return to London with the up train on the following day. The publicity to be derived from this service was so important that on 27 April, five days before the new service began operation, the LMS split the 'Royal Scot' into two portions and both ran non-stop for the 401 miles to Glasgow and the 399 miles to Edinburgh. This exercise was clearly designed solely to steal the LNER's thunder and was not repeated, particularly as the through working was well beyond the regular limits of one locomotive crew and the LMS never contemplated the construction of corridor tenders by which crew changes could be made on such a long non-stop run.

It is worth noting that during the summer of 1928 the 'Pacifics' used on the non-stop 'Flying Scotsman' service covered 125 round trips, a total of 98,165 miles, with only one late arrival and one locomotive failure – which did not lead to a late arrival!

During a visit to Doncaster Works for a General Overhaul in May 1929, No 4472 swapped her corridor tender with No 4476 *Royal Lancer*, losing tender No 5323 for the second-built corridor tender No 5324.

On 30 May 1934 No 4472 has just emerged from Doncaster Plant after a General Overhaul and is seen here on Carr Loco in a rear view that shows the details of corridor tender No 5324. *Gresley Society collection*

### The 'Flying Hamburger' and the first 100mph run in 1934

As we have seen from his Presidential address, Gresley had taken a keen interest in the high-speed 'Flying Hamburger' diesel train, reporting on its performance to the LNER Board in the spring of 1934. In that September he actually led a party visit to Germany in order to ride on the train. A decision by the LNER Board on 29 June to pursue further investigations led to details of the King's Cross to Newcastle route being supplied to the train's manufacturer, Maybach Motorenbau, with a view to an experimental service for the LNER. The results of this evaluation were disappointing, as the best overall journey times on offer were 4hr 15min in the down direction and 4hr 17min in the up.

The average speed of only 62.5mph, compared with the 77.8mph achieved in Germany, reflected

On 2 June 1934 No 4472 shares the limelight at the Ilford Exhibition with No 2001 *Cock o' the North. Ian Allan Library*

the much more demanding nature of the East Coast route, with heavy gradients and severe speed restrictions not found between Berlin and Hamburg. Equally, the diesel unit's spartan passenger accommodation for only 140 3rd Class passengers, offering only a cold buffet for refreshment, was felt to be unacceptable.

Encouraged by Wedgwood, Gresley set out to demonstrate what could be achieved by his latest 'Pacifics'. First, on Friday 30 November 1934, a high-speed test run was arranged between King's Cross and Leeds. Surprisingly, modified 'A1' 'Pacific' No 4472 *Flying Scotsman* was chosen for the train, rather than one of the new 'A3' engines. It is possible that it was the choice of driver that selected the engine, as No 4472 was the regular engine of Bill Sparshatt, who had recently been making a name for himself on the Pullman trains as a hard runner and had come to the attention of the Southern Division Locomotive Running Superintendent, I. S. W. Groom, who apparently made the selection of engine and crew for the special. Gresley held thinly disguised ambitions to make the LNER pre-eminent in locomotive speed and performance, and the return run from Leeds would give the opportunity to try for a record down Stoke bank. It was known that once the idea had been mooted, Sparshatt would need little encouragement to rise to the challenge!

To mirror the accommodation offered by its German diesel competitor, the special was only loaded to four carriages on the outward journey. The outstanding achievements on the down journey were an average speed of 90.2mph over the 24.1 miles from Hitchin to Offord, with a maximum of 94.75mph, an average speed of 82.2mph over the ascent from Helpston to Stoke, and a journey time to Leeds of 2hr 31min, a record that was destined to stand for more than 30 years until well into the diesel era. For the return up journey two more coaches were attached to the train, so an overall time of 2hr 37min was still a great achievement.

A world first was claimed, for a fully authenticated maximum speed of 100mph was recorded in the Dynamometer Car at a location between Little Bytham and Essendine that was to become more famous less than four years later. The whole round trip was made at an average speed of 72.2mph. Credit should also be paid to Bill Sparshatt's regular mate, fireman Webster. That a British steam train could equal its German diesel rival had been conclusively demonstrated.

On 4 January 1935 Wedgwood presented a paper to the LNER Board summarising the investigations to date, the results of the high-speed test of the previous November and the scope for further service accelerations. His proposals were approved and the scene was set for the second test run on 5 March 1935, a much harder task than that previously set for Sparshatt and No 4472. This time Class A3 'Pacific' No 2750 *Papyrus* was to be given the job of hauling six coaches from King's Cross to Newcastle and back on a 4-hour schedule in both directions. The outward journey, worked by Driver Gutteridge,

Before the test train to Leeds and back on 30 November 1934, Driver Sparshatt and fireman Webster are pictured at King's Cross shed preparing No 4472 for her record-breaking run. *A. Dow, Gresley Society collection*

was completed in 3 minutes inside schedule in a net time of only 3hr 50min, despite a severe delay due to a freight train derailment at Shaftholme. On the return journey Driver Sparshatt was in charge, and he managed to wind No 2750 up to a new world record maximum speed of 108mph. In fact, no fewer than four new world records were established: 12.3 miles at 100.6mph average speed; 500miles at 72.7mph average speed by one locomotive in one day with a 217-ton train; 300miles of one round trip at an average speed of 80mph; and the new maximum of 108mph. The return journey time was just under 3hr 52min gross, 3hr 48min net.

## LNER exhibition trains

Traditionally the LNER had a very effective publicity department and, as part of this activity, an extensive programme of exhibitions displaying the latest equipment and services for both passenger and freight customers. As part of this policy a series of exhibition trains toured many of the principal LNER stations throughout the 1930s, and No 4472 featured prominently at the head of many of them, only being displaced by the new 'A4' 'Pacifics' from 1935 onwards. No 4472 was photographed at Nottingham Victoria station on one such exhibition train in May 1931.

By the autumn of 1936 it was already apparent that by the following summer at least 15 of the new 'A4' 'Pacifics' would be available for service, well beyond the seven locomotives required for the three daily crack streamliner trains, and that the non-stop 'Flying Scotsman' service in the summer of 1937 could also be safely allocated to the new 'Pacifics'. Also, still being an original 180psi 'A1' class locomotive, No 4472 was, after 8½ years in top-link service, now being eclipsed for the most onerous turns by the 'A4s' and their 220psi 'A3' sisters. Accordingly, during 19/20 October 1936 No 4472 visited Doncaster Works purely for the purpose of donating her corridor tender to the new 'A4' No 4485 *Kestrel*, receiving GNR 1922-built non-corridor tender No 5290 from 'A3' No 2580 *Shotover*. Henceforward No 4472 was not to feature on the most important of the East Coast expresses, apart from occasional appearances on the winter 'Flying Scotsman' where a scheduled locomotive change at Grantham permitted use of a 'Pacific' not fitted with a corridor tender.

Another visit to Doncaster for a General Overhaul in June 1938 brought a final tender exchange, with 1936-built streamlined non-corridor tender No 5640 being acquired from No 2796 *Spearmint*. In March 1939, after 11 years of distinguished service, No 4472 was transferred from King's Cross shed to Doncaster, where she remained for most of the Second World War until a transfer after a Light Overhaul at Doncaster in February 1944 to Peterborough's New England shed a month later. As late as April 1943, during a General Overhaul at Doncaster, No 4472 lost her pre-war apple green livery, replaced by a coat of wartime austerity black with plain 'N E' lettering on the tender.

After only four months at New England, where No 4472 will undoubtedly have made a contribution to the huge southward movement of men and materials in the run-up to D-Day, a rather more interesting move took place in July 1944 to Manchester's Gorton shed. This ex-GCR shed provided locomotives for the arduous through workings between Manchester and London Marylebone via the old Great Central route through

In October 1936 No 4472 gave up her corridor tender to a new 'A4' and gained 1922 GNR tender No 5290. In this view at King's Cross shed, No 4472 is shown after regaining the original design of tender, which she retained until May 1938. *Millbrook House, KRM*

Woodhead Tunnel to Sheffield, Nottingham, Leicester and Rugby. This was of course well before the subsequent electrification of the Woodhead route, commenced by the LNER before the war but only completed by British Railways in 1955. Through locomotive workings between Manchester and Marylebone were the norm at this time, and the allocation of some 'A1' 'Pacifics' to this work in 1938 reflected the demanding nature of this particular task. Some turmoil in the allocations of LNER 'Pacifics' is apparent in late 1944, as in November No 4472 saw a return to New England for only two weeks before being transferred back to Doncaster shed three weeks later, on 5 December.

In January 1946 No 4472 was included in the locomotive renumbering scheme being implemented by the CME, Edward Thompson, initially acquiring the number 502 on 20 January 1946, revised to 103 on 5 May. It was as No 103 that the locomotive entered Doncaster Works in November 1946 for reboilering and rebuilding, emerging on 4 January 1947 with a smart new coat of apple green paint as a member of Class A3. No 103 was almost the last 'A1' (reclassified

On 8 May 1939 No 4472 has a relatively easy task heading the nine-carriage up 'Yorkshire Pullman' near Welwyn Garden City. *Ian Allan Library*

'A10' in 1944 to release 'A1' for the new Thompson 'Pacifics') to be rebuilt to Class 'A3', only a further five remaining before the last, No 60068 *Sir Visto*, emerged in December 1948. That this process of rebuilding the original 'A1' 'Pacifics' into the new standard 'A3' class had taken all of 21 years illustrates both the longevity of the original 180psi boilers and the typical LNER drive for economy in not replacing equipment while it still had some useful life left.

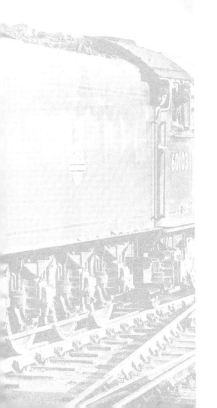

No 103 remained at Doncaster shed for a further six years, during which the railways were nationalised on 1 January 1948. Although visiting Doncaster Works for a General Overhaul in February and March 1948, No 103 still did not acquire her new BR number, simply becoming No E103 until later in 1948 when, during a Light Overhaul in late December, she emerged as No 60103. She finally exchanged her apple green livery for the new BR blue livery after a further visit to Doncaster for a General Overhaul in November and December 1949. In June 1950 No 60103 returned to the GC section with an allocation to Leicester Central shed.

For the next 2½ years No 60103 became a familiar feature of the GC main line scene, frequently being observed at the head of the 'South Yorkshireman' and 'Master Cutler' expresses between Sheffield and Marylebone, with occasional visits as far west as Manchester's London Road station. The allocation of 'Pacifics' to Leicester Central shed was not without its problems, as the shed lacked lifting facilities, so all but light maintenance had to be undertaken at Colwick shed. Also the turntable at the shed was too small, and all turning had to be

The days of the LNER are numbered as, in the summer of 1947, our locomovive, now No 103, having been renumbered in May 1946 and converted to Class A3 in January 1947, heads an up express on the GN main line. It appears that the overhaul included only a hastily repaired smokebox door. *Ian Allan Library*

undertaken at Leicester station, where there was a 70-foot turntable. Several diagrams were therefore devised to minimise turning at Leicester. One was the 1.10pm Leicester to Marylebone, returning to Leicester with the 4.50pm (both the 'South Yorkshireman') before working the down 'Master Cutler' between Leicester and Sheffield, then returning to Leicester with the 12.08am from Sheffield. Another diagram saw an 'A3' 'Pacific' work the 12.30am Leicester to Sheffield service, followed by the 7.30am 'Master Cutler' to Leicester, then the 11.30am Leicester to Marylebone, returning with the 3.20pm to Leicester.

A further General Overhaul at Doncaster in March 1952 saw No 60103 emerge in the new BR standard express passenger Brunswick green livery.

In March 1948 the newly renumbered No E103 is running in after a General Overhaul, which included acquisition of a boiler fitted with a banjo dome; she is heading a Leeds to Doncaster local service into Wakefield.
*Ian Allan Library*

From April 1953 No 60103 would also have been involved in working the 'Starlight Special' overnight reduced-fare services between Glasgow St Enoch, Edinburgh and Marylebone. Leicester 'A3s' were diagrammed to these services between Leicester and Sheffield Darnall.

November 1953 brought a return to the GN main line with reallocation back to Grantham. By now the long-distance through workings were entrusted to the Peppercorn 'A1s' and the 'A4s', leaving the shorter and less onerous duties to the 'A3s', in which Grantham shed played a prominent part. Apart from a two-month spell in 1954 back at King's Cross, No 60103 remained at Grantham for just over 3½ years before a final return to King's Cross in April 1957. Surprisingly, No 60103 had, like her original

In March 1948 the newly renumbered No E103 is running in after a General Overhaul, which included acquisition of a boiler fitted with a banjo dome; The June 1950 transfer of No 60103 to Leicester (GC) shed saw our locomotive move to a new sphere of operation. On 28 February 1953 Gorton shed has filled the tender to the brim ready for the arduous climb to Woodhead as No 60103 backs down onto the 2.10pm Manchester London Road to Marylebone express. *Eric Oldham, D. Percival collection*

In July 1957 No 60103 emerged from Doncaster Plant after a General Overhaul that included acquisition of the latest BR emblem on the tender. *D. Percival collection*

'A1' contemporaries, retained her original right-hand drive until a 1952-54 conversion programme required a special nine-day visit to Doncaster in April 1954 for conversion to the now standard left-hand drive. The return to King's Cross was occasioned by the restoration of through long-distance engine workings between London and the North, which reduced the role of Grantham shed in the principal East Coast workings.

## The fitting of Kylchap exhaust and double chimney

Despite BR Eastern Region's clear preference for the Kylchap double-chimney locomotives for use during the 1948 Locomotive Exchanges, they were surprisingly slow to seek any conversions beyond the four 'A4' locomotives delivered with this equipment in 1938 and the solitary 1937 'A3' conversion of No 2751 *Humorist*. Gresley had previously indicated that he would seek further conversions once the patent, and thus the need to pay significant royalties, had expired in 1941, but obviously the exigencies of wartime and the death of Sir Nigel, together with the antipathy of his successor Thompson towards much of the Gresley inheritance, had prevented any further developments in this direction. The Running Department had long held the view that the Kylchap cowls restricted access to the tubes for cleaning, and had resisted any further conversions. In fact, in order to minimise the risk of problems caused by shortage of steam, it became standard practice at King's Cross with every single-chimney 'A4' that had worked beyond Doncaster to have the fire thrown out on its return, the tubes rodded and the tubeplate scraped to remove any accumulation of 'bird's nests'.

That this was unnecessary on their three Kylchap 'A4s', because the blast kept the tubes clear, does not appear to have percolated through to 'official' thinking on the subject. It was to take a further nine years before the persistence of the King's Cross shedmaster, Peter Townend, eventually overcame this resistance, and on 15 May 1958 the conversion of all of the remaining 'A3s' and the 30 'A4s' was authorised. The work proceeded quickly so that No 60103 received her new Kylchap exhaust and double chimney during a visit to Doncaster for a General Overhaul in January 1959. It would be no exaggeration to state that this change totally rejuvenated all of the Gresley 'Pacifics'.

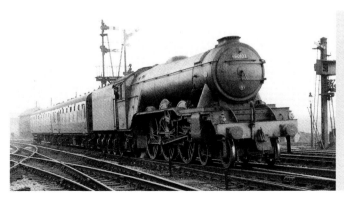

By January 1959 No 60103 had acquired a Kylchap exhaust and double chimney and is seen here at the most unlikely location of Low Moor, heading what is thought to be the Bradford portion of a Leeds to London express, usually attached at Wakefield Westgate. Sunday engineering work on the Calder Viaduct at Wakefield has required the train to take the Liversedge line at Low Moor, heading for Wakefield Kirkgate, where the Leeds portion will be attached, with No 60103 working the complete train forward to Doncaster and London. *Gresley Society collection*

The much softer exhaust produced by the fitting of the Kylchap equipment and double chimney to the 'A3s' brought a return of earlier problems experienced with No 2751 *Humorist* in the 1930s, that of drifting smoke restricting the driver's forward view. Four 'A3s' (Nos 60048, 60055, 60061 and 60112) were initially fitted with small smokebox-top deflectors similar to those previously fitted to No 2751, with similarly disappointing results. Ever the innovator, Peter Townend submitted photographs of a DB 'O1' 'Pacific' fitted with the 'trough'-type of deflector, which had been widely adopted by German Railways. A further four 'A3s' were authorised to be fitted with this type of deflector, and the first, No 60049 *Galtee More*, was loaned to King's Cross by its home shed of Grantham for a full week's test. The locomotive was put on the by now regular diesel diagram, the 10.00am King's Cross to Newcastle service, returning with the 10.10pm service. During the week's running of more than 3,000 miles, the total time that vision was obscured was 25 seconds! Accordingly, in early 1961 authority was granted for the fitting of all but four 'A3s' with this type of deflector, and some 55 were quickly equipped, many at running sheds supplied by Doncaster with a kit containing the necessary parts. No 60103 gained her German-type smoke deflectors during a visit to Doncaster for a casual repair at the end of November 1961.

The scene was now set for what many regard as the 'Indian summer' of the 'A3s' and 'A4s'. The arrival in 1958 of the first five English Electric 2,000hp diesel-electrics at King's Cross shed had marked the beginning of the end for steam, but perversely the unreliability of the new diesels presented the opportunity for the rejuvenated 'A3s' and 'A4s' to show just what they could achieve. The diagrams for the new diesels were designed to maximise the high availability of the new traction,

On 21 April 1960 No 60103 is back on GC metals to haul an Ian Allan Locospotters Special, seen here emerging from Barnstone Tunnel north of Loughborough, heading for Nottingham Victoria. *P. Groom*

In 1960 No 60103 heads the down 'Yorkshire Pullman' through the newly four-tracked Hadley Wood station. *Derek Cross*

with none of the layover times traditionally required for adequate servicing by their steam predecessors. Despite this impediment, diesel non-availability and failures ensured frequent steam substitutions, and in many cases the substitutes fulfilled the diesel diagrams with distinction. 'A4' No 60030 was recorded as having achieved 9,018 miles in 18 days of running, mainly on the 10.00am King's Cross to Newcastle and 10.10pm return. In another four-weekly period No 60030 again topped the mileage figures, achieving 11,303 miles, and as late as 1961 another 'A4' topped the four-weekly mileage charts at 11,800 miles, again higher than any of the diesels. Despite such performances, and with the increasing numbers of diesels and their gradually improving reliability, it was clear that steam was living on borrowed time. The first 'A3' had been withdrawn in December 1959, No 60104 *Solario*, none were lost in 1960, but six went in 1961, 12 in 1962 and no fewer than 33 in 1963. The Kylchap-fitted 'A3s' were now used turn and turn about with the 'A4s', with similar performances being daily delivered.

The early unreliability of the new diesels required many steam substitutions on the cyclic diagrams designed for the diesels, which required an intensity

In December 1961 No 60103 had acquired the German-type trough smoke deflectors to emerge in her final BR condition. Here on 14 June 1962 No 60103, in sparkling condition, presumably deputising for a failed diesel, hauls a down local south of Wood Green. *P. Groom*

On 28 July 1962 the tables had been turned as, after failing at Hitchin the previous day on the 1.00pm Harrogate to King's Cross train, No 60103 is ignominiously hauled through Stevenage back to King's Cross by 'Baby Deltic' No D5908. *D. Percival*

of working never previously attempted with steam. Return trips to Newcastle within 12 hours became normal, and if necessary back to Newcastle again within a few hours. As late as 1961 the four-weekly mileage returns showed the highest mileage of any King's Cross-allocated locomotive was not one of the new diesels, but a 36-year-old Gresley 'Pacific'.

No 60103 made her last BR-sponsored visit to Doncaster Works for a General Overhaul in May 1962. The English Electric 2,000hp diesels had now been supplemented by the 22 3,300hp 'Deltics', and the writing was truly on the wall for steam. After BR had decided not to include No 60103 in its formal list of locomotives to be preserved, various efforts emerged to privately acquire the locomotive, which achieved their culmination in January 1963. No 60103 worked her last BR train, the 1.15pm King's Cross to Leeds, as far as Doncaster on

14 January. After a well-attended high-profile media event at King's Cross, the journey north proceeded without incident, apart from passing No 60007 *Sir Nigel Gresley* working the 12.45 Hull to King's Cross service at Claypole. Arrival at Doncaster was 6 minutes early, just as the up 'White Rose' passed, enabling an exchange of whistles with its locomotive, No 60022 *Mallard*.

After retiring to within the confines of her birthplace almost 40 years earlier, Doncaster Plant, No 60103 was quietly withdrawn from BR service on 15 January, not to follow the ultimate fate of all of her sister 'A1s' and 'A3s' and be scrapped, but to be transferred to the ownership of Mr Alan Pegler, who had accompanied the locomotive on the footplate for her last BR journey.

On a snowy 14 January 1963 No 60103 hauled her last BR train, the 1.15pm King's Cross to Leeds, as far as Doncaster. Here prior to departure from King's Cross her new owner Alan Pegler proudly stands on the front of the engine before riding on the footplate throughout the journey. Note that Alan is sporting a Festiniog Railway cap badge. *A. Dow collection, Gresley Society*

No 60103's last BR train makes a steamy exit from King's Cross.
*Ian Allan Library*

**A**lan Pegler was a businessman with family interests in Doncaster and with The Northern Rubber Company at Retford. He was also a prominent railway enthusiast, President of the Gainsborough Model Railway Club, and organiser of a number of special trains during the 1950s, including the 'Centenaries Express' of 1952 and the 'Plant Centenarian' in 1953. In 1954 he was invited to join the Eastern Area Board of the British Transport Commission. This gave Alan privileged access to key personalities at BTC headquarters, including the officer responsible for drawing up the list of steam locomotives to be preserved, Terry Miller. Of the LNER Gresley 'Pacifics', only *Mallard* was listed, as the ultimate design and world speed record holder. Alan failed to get *Flying Scotsman* included in the list, but from his discussions with Terry Miller emerged an agreement in principle at the end of 1962 to undertake a complete overhaul of the then No 60103, prior to sale for the then not inconsiderable sum of £3,000. The Gresley A3 Preservation Society was already actively raising funds for the acquisition of No 60103; having been

The first public trip in preservation for No 4472 was on 20 April 1963 when she hauled the Festiniog Railway Society's AGM Special from Paddington to Ruabon, returning overnight from Shrewsbury. Here the train leaves Paddington. *R. C. Riley*

pipped at the post by Alan Pegler for the locomotive, the society became The Gresley Society and instead acquired the only Gresley tank locomotive to be preserved, 'N2' No 69523 (at present running as GNR No 1744), of which I am currently the caretaker.

The work of restoration began almost immediately after formal withdrawal, and by 7 February the Kylchap exhaust, double chimney and German-style smoke deflectors had all been removed, restoring the locomotive to close to her original appearance. The 1936-built streamlined-type non-corridor tender No 5640, to which she had been coupled since July 1938, was swapped with a corridor tender from the original 1928 batch, No 5325, formerly belonging to No 60034 *Lord Faringdon*. This tender had not previously run behind No 4472, being attached first to No 2573 in 1928, to No 2564 between 1928 and 1935, No 2506 between 1935 and 1936, then 'A4s' Nos 4488 and 60033 before being attached to No 60034 in 1954. By 29 March work had progressed sufficiently for a test run to be

undertaken over the classic LNER testing route of Doncaster to Barkston Junction and back. Resuming her old LNER identity as No 4472, and with a new coat of apple green livery, the locomotive looked very smart.

On 14 June 1963 the return 'Great Central Railtour' from Sheffield Victoria to Marylebone passes New Basford approaching Nottingham Victoria.
*T. Boustead, Millbrook House*

On 18 April 1964 No 4472 worked another 'Great Central Railtour', this time throughout from Marylebone to Manchester Central. For the passage through the new Woodhead Tunnel an electric pilot was required, and here we see No 4472 at Dunford Bridge about to attach EM1 Bo-Bo No 26051 for the passage through the tunnel. Alan Pegler is in the foreground between the locomotives. *Gresley Society collection*

As subsequent events proved, the Sale Agreement, a copy of which I have seen, signed with BR on 16 April, was far-sighted, including a three-year running and maintenance agreement (later extended to 1968, then 1971) and giving contractually guaranteed access to the BR network, the only steam locomotive to enjoy this right. Also included in the Agreement was provision for a new home for the locomotive in the old engine weigh house just off the southern end of No 8 platform at Doncaster, with a lease at a rate of £65 per annum. The former Secretary of the Gainsborough Model Railway Club, George Hinchcliffe, was recruited as Locomotive Manager, ably supported by a small group of former railwaymen and members of the GMRC.

Among Alan Pegler's many railway interests, he had led the group that had obtained control of the Festiniog Railway in North Wales, so it was entirely appropriate that No 4472's first public main-line trip in her new career was heading the Festiniog Railway Society's AGM Special from Paddington to Ruabon on 20 April 1963. Appropriately again, the second charter to be undertaken by No 4472 was for the Gainsborough Model Railway Club, on 18 May, from Doncaster to Southampton via the Great Central route. This was followed on 14 June 1963 by a rail tour from Marylebone over the remains of the Great Central main line, with the locomotive being serviced at the London end at the former Midland depot at Cricklewood. A celebrity guest visit to the Eastleigh Works Open Day was then made on 21 August.

In 1964 Alan Pegler had a private charter on 18 March from Doncaster to Cardiff with a three-coach train including a former 'Devon Belle' Pullman Observation Car. This was for a presentation to Alan, as Chairman of the Festiniog Railway Company, by

After the Darlington overhaul on 10 April 1965, a 'thank you' special was run to Peterborough and back for works staff and their families. Here the train is accelerating up Dalton bank away from Darlington on the outward journey, with Alan Pegler in the fireman's seat.
*Chris Nettleton*

the Wales Tourist Board. A charter for the SLS on 18 April took No 4472 from Manchester Central via the Woodhead route to Sheffield and the Great Central route to Marylebone and back. No 4472 probably became the first steam locomotive to work a passenger train through the new Woodhead Tunnel, reserved exclusively for electric trains since its formal opening in June 1954. For the passage through the tunnel between Dunford Bridge and Woodhead stations in both directions No 4472 was required to take Class EM1 Bo-Bo electric locomotive No 26051 as pilot. On 2 May No 4472 worked a Gresley Society special from Doncaster to Darlington and back, which had been brought from King's Cross by No 60106 *Flying Fox*.

On 9 May 1964 No 4472 headed the appropriately named 'Pegler Pullman' from Doncaster to Edinburgh, returning with No 60009. This utilised the 'Master Cutler' set in order to position the locomotive so that she could pose on 11 May for a painting by the famous artist Terence Cuneo on the Forth Bridge. The next trip was on 16 May, a charter for the University of St Andrews Railway and Transport Society from

Edinburgh to Aberdeen and back. On 16 August No 4472 worked a circuitous charter from Sheffield to Eastleigh via the Lickey incline, Gloucester and Swindon. A promotional trip for ice-cream maker Lyons Maid, the 'Zoom Special', took No 4472 from York to King's Cross and back on 30 August, then on 12 September she worked the first of several 'Farnborough Flyer' charters to the Farnborough Air Show. On 3 October No 4472 worked a return special from King's Cross to Darlington, outward via Harrogate and Ripon and returning direct via York. This trip was unusual in that from Harrogate to Darlington and back to York No 4472 was assisted by the privately owned Gresley 'K4' 2-6-0 No 3442 *The Great Marquess*, which had worked her own train from Leeds to Harrogate before both trains were combined forward to York, where No 3442 was detached. On 19 October Ian Allan sponsored an all-Pullman special from Paddington to Ilfracombe, and at the end of that month a King's Cross to York return trip was run.

By now it was clear that the locomotive required further works attention. Doncaster Works was finished with any steam overhaul work, so a first visit to Darlington Works took place in early 1965. During the overhaul No 4472 had a boiler change, acquiring 1944-built boiler No 27020 from No 60041 *Salmon Trout*. An initial test run was made, hauling a single goods brake-van, on 23 February, on a circular route from Darlington to Eaglescliffe, Stockton, Sunderland and Newcastle before returning to Darlington. No 4472 featured in an Open Day at Darlington Works on 3 April before finally emerging on 10 April to haul a special 'thank you' train formed of the 'Tees-Tyne Pullman' stock and Pullman Observation Car to Peterborough and back for 110 Darlington Works staff. One significant change that dates from this visit is that No 4472 acquired a Darlington trademark – green-painted cylinder covers.

The 1965 return to traffic was celebrated in appropriate style with a Paddington to Gobowen charter on 9 May for the Anglo-Norse Society. On 29 May No 4472 worked the 'East Midlander No 6 Railtour' for the RCTS from Nottingham to Swindon and back via Clapham Junction! In September two trips were sponsored by the GMRS on consecutive days, on the 11th from Doncaster to Kensington Olympia via the Midland Main Line, and on the 12th from Waterloo to Weymouth, returning via Yeovil to Paddington. October brought the first significant casualty when, on the 9th, a *Railway Magazine*-sponsored Paddington to Cardiff high-speed special was brought to a premature end at Swindon with No 4472 displaying a leaking left-hand steamchest cover. The train was rescued by 'Hymek' diesel-hydraulic No 7089. Honour was restored just

On 13 November 1965 No 4472 returns the WWF 'Panda Pullman' from Cardiff to Paddington climbing out of the Severn Tunnel through Patchway. *D. McIntosh*

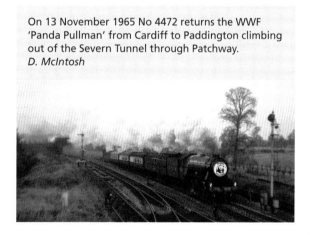

During the course of a trip to Inverkeithing on 16 April 1966 No 4472's return journey was via the Waverley route and the S&C. Here on the return journey she climbs through Stobs, north of Hawick on the Waverley route. *D. C. Williams*

over a month later when, on 13 November, No 4472 worked a triumphant five-coach return trip from Paddington to Cardiff for the World Wildlife Fund, called the 'Panda Pullman'.

Further trips early in 1966 included, on 8 January, a Doncaster to March and return private trip for Alan Pegler, then a tour from St Pancras to King's Cross via Leicester and Sheffield on the 18th. March was planned to be occupied by an exhibition train visit to the National Trades Technical Society Exhibition at Sheffield, but this was cancelled. April began with a trip on the 16th from Northallerton to Inverkeithing via Sunderland. On 1 May there was another Anglo-Norse Society trip, this time from Peterborough to York and back, followed a week later by a GMRS trip from Birmingham to Spalding for the Flower Parade.

June 1966 saw two trips, the first on the 4th being a GMRS trip from Lincoln to Llandudno. This was typical of trips undertaken at this time, and it is worth noting that departure was at 5.50am, running via Doncaster, Wakefield Kirkgate,

On 17 September 1966 No 4472 climbs up to the Grosvenor Bridge over the River Thames en route to Brighton. *P. Groom*

The first trip utilising the newly acquired second tender was the 'Elizabethan' from King's Cross to Newcastle on 22 October 1966. Here the train leaves Welwyn North Tunnel and approaches Woolmer Green. *D. Percival*

to Edinburgh via Carlisle and the Waverley route, returning via the East Coast route to Doncaster. On 10 September there was another GMRS 'Farnborough Flyer', before a trip from Victoria to Brighton and back on the 17th. October saw two trips, a first outing for the second tender on a further GMRS Lincoln to Blackpool trip on the 8th, followed on the 22nd by an ARES 'Elizabethan' charter that took No 4472 on a King's Cross to York round trip, worked forward to Newcastle and back by Merchant Navy class No 35026 *Lamport and Holt Line*, a late substitute for a non-available 'A4'.

Extensive operation of the locomotive on a network that had either already abandoned steam traction or was rapidly preparing to end the regular use of steam brought the realisation that the basic requirements for servicing steam locomotives were fast disappearing, particularly water troughs and columns. Accordingly, in April 1966, at a cost of £800, a second tender was acquired, No 5332 from No 60009, another of the 1928-built corridor type. This was then modified at Doncaster Works to carry 5,600 gallons of water while still retaining the

Huddersfield, Manchester Victoria and Chester, arriving at Llandudno at 11.00am. The return journey commenced at 8.05pm and eventually arrived back in Lincoln at 1.35am on the Sunday morning. Then on the 25th the task was to haul a WRS charter originating at Waterloo from Hellifield 'walk-through' facility. After a trial run on 3 October over the traditional Doncaster to Barkston route, this second tender was regularly coupled behind the existing vehicle. At the same time the locomotive number was taken from the cab sides and put on the rear tender. On the cab sides the number was replaced by metal plates carrying the LNER coat of arms, in a very similar fashion to that carried by the locomotive during and after the Wembley Exhibition in 1924/25.

Also some shortcomings in the old Doncaster weigh house home were becoming apparent,

On 30 April 1967 No 4472 crosses a King's Cross to Chesterfield special from the down slow to the down fast line at Cadwell signal box. *D. Percival*

particularly access for maintenance and coaling, so negotiations began over a possible relocation to the Old Fitting Shop at Doncaster Carr Loco at a revised rental of £100 per annum. This was finally achieved in March 1968, the former home of No 4472 since 1963 being then needed for an abortive scheme to house No 4771 *Green Arrow*, which was to be looked after by Doncaster Corporation. Arrangements were also made for regular supplies of Yorkshire Main Colliery washed cobbles to be supplied to Carr Loco, a typical 13-tonne wagon load in 1967 costing £85.

April and May 1967 saw further trips to and from King's Cross and Norwich before a busy three months that included another Gainsborough Railway Society charter, the 'Retford Rover', on 21 May, before a *Railway Magazine*-sponsored 'Hadrian Flyer' attempted non-stop run from King's Cross to

The return 'Retford Rover' on 21 May 1967 is seen near Brookman's Park. *Ian Allan Library*

Newcastle on 17 June, returning behind 'Deltic' No D9005. The non-stop run was frustrated by a points failure at Tuxford, which caused a 37-minute delay. This was followed by a 'Scunthorpe Forum Flyer' from Doncaster to Edinburgh on 25 June. An Arts Festival at Chester in July provided the opportunity for exhibition of No 4472 at that city with the preserved No 4498 *Sir Nigel Gresley* before a Chester to Blackpool return charter on 9 July. A boiler inspection took place on 8 August, which required the replacement of one copper stay.

At this time it is clear from the BR records that some concerns were being expressed regarding aspects of the running of the locomotive. Initial concerns were raised regarding a planned September working through Stockport under the 25kV overhead power supplies. This revealed that on previous occasions No 4472 had visited Doncaster Works to have the locomotive springs screwed down to reduce its overall height to 13ft 1½in, a return visit being required to restore the original spring set-up after the trip. Consultation with the LMR revealed that the overhead line

On 9 July 1967 No 4472 climbs out of Chester towards Guilden Sutton with the 'Chester Festival Flyer' to Blackpool. *D. McIntosh*

equipment (OHLE) north of Crewe had a minimum clearance of 13ft 6in, so this practice had been totally unnecessary! The locomotive had been required to carry OHLE warning flashes since February 1966.

I have seen minutes of a meeting held at the York HQ of the Eastern Region on 24 August 1967 to discuss concerns regarding operation of the locomotive. An interesting and very positive paper was presented by the Divisional Manager Norwich, which, although anonymous, was I believe written by David Ward, later to become the BR steam supremo. Further concerns were raised in September 1967 after the preserved Gresley 'Pacific' No 4498 *Sir Nigel Gresley* had started several lineside fires between Grantham and Newark during the course of a Peterborough to Newcastle trip. The correspondence revealed that all privately owned steam locomotives were required to carry their own insurance cover, with the sole exception of No 4472, where BR was liable for any lineside fires!

September and October 1967 saw three separate trips to or from Norwich or Ipswich, the last, on the 14th, being worked by No 4498. A further ARES charter from St Pancras to Leicester, returning from Sheffield to King's Cross, the 'Palatine', was run on 18 November. Also in November the BRB had announced a complete ban on the operation of privately owned locomotives, beyond that already agreed. Alan Pegler's running agreement for No 4472 had previously been extended to 1971, so shortly afterwards No 4472 became the only preserved steam locomotive able to operate on the national network.

1968 proved to be another busy and rather special year for No 4472. On 28 February she undertook a test run from Doncaster to Newcastle and return to evaluate coal and water consumption prior to a London to Edinburgh trip planned for May. On 15 March a charter was worked from Doncaster to Stockport for an Open Day at Stockport Edgeley shed on the 16th, which also featured No 70013 *Oliver Cromwell* and preserved No 5596 *Bahamas*. This was followed on the 17th by two Stockport to Carnforth return charters for Williams Deacons Bank, hauled by No 4472 and No 70013 respectively. On 18 March No 4472 worked a trip from Stockport back to Doncaster. On 23 March she ran from King's Cross to Keighley and back, followed on 6 April by a WRS Doncaster-Scarborough-Sheffield trip on a train originating in Birmingham. This acted as a taster prior to the recreation on 1 May 1968 of the first non-stop King's Cross to Edinburgh run made by No 4472

On 1 May 1968 No 4472 crosses the Royal Border Bridge over the River Tweed at Berwick with the non-stop 40th Anniversary Special. *Derek Cross*

exactly 40 years earlier. With the assistance of the second tender, the non-stop run was achieved, albeit a very close run thing when delayed by a broken rail at Bentley, signals at Manors, and being looped at Berwick to facilitate a water stop from an adjacent tanker. As the water was not required, the train progressed slowly along the loop until the offending signal cleared at the very last minute. The journey was completed in just under 8 hours, arriving only 5 minutes late. A return trip on 4 May was completed non-stop without problems in 7hr 35min, arriving 2 minutes early.

Fortunately No 4472's second main-line failure in preservation took place soon after the non-stop recreation, on 25 May during a Darlington to Edinburgh and return trip. The locomotive failed at Morpeth on the return journey with a burst tube and had to be rescued by 'Deltic' No D9007.

On 25 May 1968 No 4472 worked from Darlington to Edinburgh and is seen here departing from Waverley with the return working. *Derek Cross*

Repairs were undertaken at Gateshead shed before a return to Doncaster. This inevitably raised questions regarding the state of No 4472's tubes, and arrangements began to be made for a full retube to be undertaken later in the year.

From 11 August 1968, with the end of regular BR steam-hauled services, No 4472 became the only steam locomotive operating on the national network, with the sole exception of the narrow-gauge Vale of Rheidol line. On 7 September an SLS/MRS special was hauled from Huddersfield to Tyne Dock and return, which required light engine movements from Doncaster to Huddersfield via Sheffield and Penistone in both directions. On 14 September No 4472 working from Norwich to Chesterfield and back, then on the 29th she worked another special for the GMRS, this time from Retford to Tyseley for the depot Open Day. While at Tyseley No 4472 was used to work a return trip from Tyseley to Leamington Spa. Three trips were worked in quick succession in early October: on the 4th a schools special from Doncaster to King's Cross, followed on the 6th by a 'Yorkshire Harvester' return

trip from King's Cross to York and, on the 7th, a return home at the head of a schools charter from Potters Bar to York. Then on the 20th a return trip from Leeds to King's Cross was followed on the 26th by 'The Moorlander' from Liverpool to Carlisle, outwards via Shap and back via the Settle & Carlisle line, Leeds and Huddersfield. After the tube failure in May concerns were being expressed regarding the condition of the other tubes, and discussions commenced regarding repairs. In November 1968 No 4472 entered the Leeds Works of the Hunslet Engine Company for an overhaul.

In 1965 *The Railway Magazine* had carried the first suggestion of an American visit for No 4472, then in November 1967 Alan Pegler had visited New York, Chicago, Washington and Green Bay, when a tour in 1968 had been discussed. During 1967 the American President of Campbells Soups had also approached Alan Pegler with the idea of a 12-month British Trade Mission tour of Canada and the United States, during which the locomotive would both haul trains and be the main feature in several Trade Fairs promoting British goods. There was support but, significantly, no formal backing from the Board of Trade, which, as discussions progressed through 1968, became more circumspect.

While in Hunslet's works in Leeds the locomotive was inspected, in accordance with the prevailing convention, by officials from the first North American railway planned to host the locomotive, at this stage the Canadian National Railway. The plan was for the locomotive to travel by sea to Montreal before travelling to Boston. After emerging from Hunslet's on 26 January No 4472 worked a 12-coach empty test train from Doncaster to Newcastle and back. Moving south on 8 February, on the 22nd she worked from St Pancras to Cleethorpes with a 'mystery' excursion. Leaking superheater element joints caused a failure at Cleethorpes, followed by

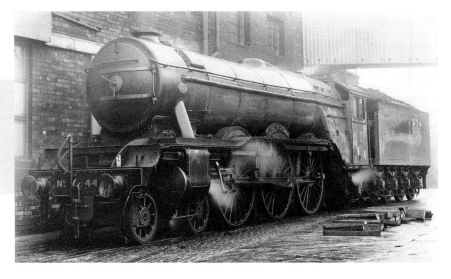

During early 1969 No 4472 visited the Hunslet Engine Co in Leeds for an overhaul. She is seen here on arrival in the works before dismantling began. *D. Percival*

A fine panning shot of No 4472 at speed leaving Hadley Wood Tunnel with a down special on 31 August 1969. *P. Groom*

another similar failure at Thursby on 1 March with a return King's Cross to Cleethorpes trip.

Discussions followed with Hunslet over remedial action, which was undertaken at Doncaster, after which BR required a further Doncaster to Newcastle test run. This was successfully completed before, on 30 March 1969, No 4472 worked a special from King's Cross to Leicester via Cambridge, then, on 4 May, a special for the RCTS from Grantham to Tyseley and back via Leicester and Nuneaton. On 10 May No 4472 was back in Edinburgh, followed on the 17th by a King's Cross to Diss 'Norfolkman' return trip. On 21 June she worked a return mystery excursion from Huddersfield to Cleethorpes via

Penistone and Lincoln. A 29 June circular 'North Eastern' special for the NELPG from Newcastle via York and Leeds to Keighley, returning via Carlisle, was so successful that it was repeated on 1 July.

In 1969 plans for the North American visit were initially postponed by an American longshoremen's strike, but were later finalised to the extent that on 6 July No 4472 entered Doncaster Works for the fitting of American-style whistle and cowcatcher, a warning bell donated by the US Southern Railway, and buckeye couplers. After trial fitting, these items, apart from the bell, were temporarily removed for two trips on 14 August from Doncaster to March and Peterborough, returning direct to Doncaster, and on 31 August from King's Cross to Newcastle and return. This was promoted as 'Flying Scotsman's last trip before USA visit'.

Later the same day No 4472 is being serviced at York before the return journey to London. Note the large US-style chime whistle and bell, fitted in preparation for the North America tour.
*Gresley Society*

n what was partly a positioning movement for the Newcastle trip, on 18 August 1969 No 4472 worked vehicles from Doncaster to Hornsey and Twickenham before returning to Hornsey. Then on 18 September she moved back to Twickenham, where the exhibition train vehicles were being fitted out. The complete exhibition train was formed of nine vehicles. First was admin car BCK 21177, then reception car BCK E104 followed by four exhibition cars, E70636/ E70632/ E70758/ E70497, and Pullman cars *Isle of Thanet* and *Lydia* with, at the rear, former 'Devon Belle' Pullman Observation Car No SC281. This final vehicle, purchased by Alan Pegler in 1968, had to be registered in the United States as the 'Flying Scotsman Club' in order to comply with United States liquor laws.

At 1545 on 19 September 1969 No 4472 departed from Twickenham working a train of four vehicles, including the two Pullman cars, overnight via Cricklewood, Sheffield, Wakefield, Huddersfield and Manchester Victoria to Liverpool Edge Hill. I was privileged to accompany No 4472 throughout this journey, and

I still treasure a footplate recording made during the climb from Huddersfield to Diggle in the early hours of the 20th. On arrival at Edge Hill No 4472 was moved down to Canada Dock for loading the same day by the MDHB floating crane *Mammoth* on to the deck of the Cunard liner *Saxonia* for passage to Boston. The five exhibition cars had been worked separately from Twickenham to Liverpool Docks. The tour had also been finally amended to delete the initial visit to Montreal and Canada, and was now to commence in Boston.

The British-flagged *Saxonia* was a typical cargo liner of 5,586grt, built in 1964 at South Shields, a type of vessel soon to disappear as a result of the container revolution. She left Cunard's North Atlantic services in 1970, transferring to the Cunard-Brocklebank Line's services to the Arabian Gulf and Indian Ocean as *Maharonda* before being laid up in 1977 in the River Fal. She was later sold to Singapore owners and renamed as the *New Deer*, finally being scrapped in China in 1983. She arrived in Boston and unloaded her precious cargo at noon on Sunday 28 September.

Before the North American tour could take place a number of significant administrative hurdles had to be overcome. A vacuum-braked steam locomotive and train to designs alien to the USA would normally have been banned from operation, as the organisations that later attempted to import to the USA steam locomotives from China would confirm. Despite this, Alan Pegler sought and obtained clearance to operation the train from both the Interstate Commerce Commission (ICC) and the Association of American Railroads (AAR). Despite the financial turmoil that most US railroads were experiencing at the time, satisfactory arrangements were made with a variety of host lines for the initial planned tours from Boston to Houston, Texas, and thence to Green Bay, Wisconsin.

The total exhibition train shipped to the USA consisted of nine vehicles, the five exhibition vans plus a Mk 1 brake, the two Pullman Cars and the former 'Devon Belle' Observation Car. A variety of British companies took space in the exhibition cars and the overall objective was to entertain potential customers and win new orders during a programme that was to be spread over 12 months, during which all major conurbations would be visited. The first tour was to take six weeks in the autumn of 1969, and was scheduled to take the locomotive and train from Boston to Houston in Texas, a distance of 2,145 miles. Generally tours were planned so that between exhibitions the locomotive would haul the train around 300 miles daily, usually without any assistance except over the most severe gradients, with overnight stops at convenient locations. North American railroadmen, more used to refuelling every 100 miles and to seeing clouds of smoke, soon realised that No 4472 was amazingly economical and went about her business in a modest but highly professional manner! Operationally the tour was a great success, with the active assistance and support of many key professional railroad executives, particularly the notable steam fan Graham Claytor, then CEO of the Southern Railway and later to become CEO of Amtrak. Claytor was also responsible for the donation of the locomotive bell that was to adorn No 4472 for the duration of her North America tour, fitted during the Doncaster Works visit in July.

After being unloaded from *Saxonia* on 28 September, the train was moved for assembly to the Army base terminal in Boston. By 3 October No 4472 was ready for a successful 240-mile test run over former New Haven tracks to New London, via Providence and Mystic River. One pleasant surprise was that No 4472 appeared to steam well on the Southern West Virginia coal supplied, and this was therefore used throughout the run to Houston. An overall speed limit of 45mph was applied to the train throughout the tour, and No 4472 responded well to this generally undemanding task virtually without incident.

Four days later, on 7 October, the train was hauled by No 4472 from the Army base to Boston's South station, ready for the tour's opening ceremony to be held the following day. About an hour before the ceremony, the locomotive was taken out of sight, then, to the sound of bagpipes, was backed on to the train at exactly 10.00am. Thus was set the scene for what eventually proved to be a very eventful time in the life of No 4472.

The list of US railroads that hosted No 4472 and her train now reads like a list of 'fallen flags', such have been the wide changes and consolidation that have taken place in US railroading during the last 40 years. The tour then began over the then Penn Central main line across Massachusetts, Rhode Island and Connecticut to New Rochelle, some 16 miles short of New York. Although travelling under the 11,000V dc overhead electric wires of the former New York, New Haven & Hartford Railroad from New Haven onwards, only when approaching New York was a pilot locomotive required, in accordance with NY smoke abatement regulations. One of the ex-Pennsylvania Railroad's famous 'GG-1' electric locomotives, No 4857, was attached in order to haul a now fire-dropped No 4472 and train for the last few miles via the Hellgate Bridge into New York's Pennsylvania station. As smoke abatement regulations had banned steam locomotives from City precincts since the early years of the 20th century, *Flying Scotsman* may have been the very first steam locomotive to enter the present station.

After a couple of days on exhibition, the train was again electrically hauled some 5 miles through the Hudson Tunnel to Meadows yard in New Jersey. Here steam was again raised ready for the next stage of the journey south on 18 October, over the former Pennsylvania electrified main line to Philadelphia. After taking on coal and water at Philadelphia, the train continued a further 95 miles on Penn Central tracks to Baltimore, Maryland. It was during this stage that the first technical problem emerged when a regulator gland packing blew out, necessitating taking the locomotive out of steam in order that the gland could be repacked. After a day on exhibition in Baltimore the train departed on 26 October for the short 38-mile haul to Washington DC, assisted by another 'GG-1' electric, No 4845, where again coal and water were replenished.

Leaving Washington on 29 October the train briefly used the tracks of the historic 'bridge' line, the Richmond, Fredericksburg & Potomac Railroad, before gaining the tracks of the Southern Railway at Alexandria. There was then a long haul over the

SR's main line across Virginia through Lynchburg, then across the Carolinas through Charlotte to the centre of the Southern system at Atlanta, before continuing over Southern Railway tracks to Anniston and Birmingham, Alabama. The highlight of this section of the tour on 2 November was a hugely successful 'meet' at Anniston, which was estimated to have been attended by some 10,000 people, with two of the principal locomotives featuring in the then very active steam programme of the Southern Railway. These were No 750, a beautifully finished green and gold-liveried Alco 4-6-2 of 1910. This locomotive started life as Florida East Coast No 80, being sold to the Southern constituent Savannah & Atlanta in 1935 before being donated to the Atlanta Chapter of the National Railroad Historical Society (NHRS) in 1962. The other was No 4501, an 'M' class 2-8-2 built by Baldwin in 1911 for the Southern Railway and preserved by the Tennessee Valley Railroad at Chattanooga.

At New Haven, alongside New Haven RR electro-diesel FL9 No 5045.
*H . A. Edmonson*

Proceeding on 4 November from Birmingham, the train passed through Meridian in Mississippi, leaving Southern Railway metals for the tracks of Illinois Central via Jackson and Vicksburg to Monroe, then Shreveport in Louisiana. A further railroad that was now joined for a relatively short haul was the Texas & Pacific, for 182 miles to Dallas, Texas. The Texas & Pacific was famous among other things for its former fleet of 70 magnificent 2-10-4 'Texas'-type locomotives. In complete contrast to the crowds experienced at Anniston, the people of Dallas, one of the largest cities in the world without a passenger rail service, refused to believe that there was a train in the former station and numbers were well below expectations. After a day's stop in Fort Worth, the train proceeded over the tracks of the joint CB&Q and CRI&P ('Rock Island') line to an overnight stop at Aldine, some 12 miles from Houston. Approximately 100 miles from Houston, No 4472 experienced only the second mechanical

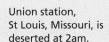
Union station, St Louis, Missouri, is deserted at 2am.

problem encountered thus far on the tour, a fractured left-hand cylinder lubrication pipe. This did not slow progress and was quickly repaired during the overnight stop. On 10 November the train moved on again to Houston, arriving to a great reception precisely on time at 10.23am. After a week's display the train was put into store in north-west Texas, just south of Lubbock, at Slaton.

Despite all the early enthusiasm, once in the USA it became apparent that insufficient preparation and advance marketing had been undertaken. In addition, looking back over 40 years, it is important to remember that railways were not then the resurgent means of transport they are today. By the end of the 1960s most USA railroads had run down or abandoned their passenger services and only a few surviving services struggled on before being rescued by the publicly owned national passenger network operator Amtrak in 1971. At this time train-riding in the USA was only for the most determined, and the general public had learned from bitter experience to hate trains. Against the background of the slow and unpopular death of the North American passenger train, the perceived instigators of this decline, the railroad companies, had a very poor public image. Most of the surviving railroad stations were run-down, unattractive places unlikely to attract visitors, and the insularity of the American public was something of a shock to the tour team. To the general public of the USA the name *Flying Scotsman* meant very little if anything at all and, combined with little advance marketing, it proved very difficult to attract crowds to the train. In addition to attracting business customers to the exhibition train, a key feature of the business plan was to raise income by retailing souvenirs, for which large crowds were a prerequisite. There were also problems with the incompatibility of the train's UK electrics with the standard US system, and with the internal layout of the exhibition carriages not facilitating the passage of visitors through the train. Some exhibitors wished to entertain a wide range of potential customers, some wished merely to entertain invited guests, some wished customers to spend time examining products at leisure, while others wanted a rapid through-flow of visitors. With the very mixed financial results of the first tour, future progress required careful reconsideration and planning. Few of the exhibitors were confident enough to finance further tours, overheads had proved to be unexpectedly high, and it was obvious that the big US cities were not the ideal venue for a British exhibition train.

However, the agreement to use the two Pullman cars in the train was conditional on an undertaking to deliver *Isle of Thanet* to the US National Railroad Museum at Green Bay, Wisconsin, so this was an obligation to be delivered.

By the spring of 1970 George Hinchcliffe, having retired from the teaching profession and become the Managing Director of Flying Scotsman Enterprises, set out with a small team to devise a workable solution to the problem. George had been convinced during the first tour that by reorienting the exhibition towards the general public, rather than businessmen, and by visiting smaller places with good advance media coverage, it would be possible for the train to pay its way. Accordingly a second tour was planned for 1970 to move the train and the Pullman cars the 3,500

miles from Slaton, Texas, to Green Bay, Wisconsin, and on to Montreal. The train was reconfigured so that visitors entered via the locomotive footplate, passed through the corridor tender, visited all the coaches and left through the rear vehicle. This proved to be a much more satisfactory arrangement, the visiting crowds were kept moving and a carefully placed souvenir stand did a roaring trade. For example, at the small town of Lomesa, Texas, there were 1,500 visitors in 2 hours, and the box office took enough money to finance a good part of the tour and encourage all concerned that there was the prospect of better things to come.

Leaving Slaton on 14 June 1970 was by means of two Santa Fe subsidiaries, the Panhandle & Santa Fe to Sweetwater, a few miles west of Abilene, then continuing over Gulf, Colorado & Pacific tracks to Temple, before joining the tracks of a new host railway, the Missouri-Kansas-Texas Railroad (the KATY) on to Waco. A minor derailment at Waco caused a 24-hour delay before the next movement to Dallas. The route then continued on KATY tracks via Dallas, leaving on 18 June, to Dennison and across Oklahoma and Kansas to Kansas City, then forward on the 30th through Fulton to St Louis, for a stop of five days to 6 July. Then the forward route was by Norfolk & Western tracks to Decatur and Chicago, over the route of the famous Wabash 'Blue Bird' Vistadome express, to the now long-abandoned former Santa Fe station at Dearborn in Chicago, for a ten-day stay between 8 and 18 July.

Leaving Chicago on the 18th was over the tracks of yet another new railroad, the Chicago North Western, along the shores of Lake Michigan across Wisconsin and through Milwaukee to Green Bay. Here the Pullman car *Isle of Thanet* was successfully delivered to the National Railroad Museum and there was enough money in the bank to keep the train moving on to Montreal. Leaving Green Bay on 25 August, the train retraced its steps to Milwaukee and Chicago before following Penn Central tracks to South Bend and Detroit. Crossing into Canada at Windsor, Ontario, the route was then over CN tracks via London, Kingston and Niagara Falls to Toronto Unfortunately, receipts in Canada proved a great disappointment. Despite a guaranteed exhibition fee

at the Canadian National Exhibition in Toronto, souvenir sales (which made the difference between break-even and profit) slumped badly. In a distinct contrast, after moving along the coast of Lake Ontario to Kingston the stay proved to be a great financial success, helped by an excellent lakeside position obtained through the cooperation of the Harbour Master. Montreal on 29/30 August brought further disappointment, however, and the locomotive and train then returned to Toronto for winter storage within the CN Spadina roundhouse, alongside the preserved CN 4-8-4 No 6218.

Further deliberations were required, and while in Toronto a meeting with the CEO of the Canadian Pacific Railway brought forward an offer to help move the locomotive and train to Vancouver. Interestingly, this meeting was joined by British MP Nicholas Ridley. Unfortunately, since the election of the Heath Government in 1970 the Department for Trade and Industry had adopted a very negative attitude towards the image of a steam locomotive in promoting British exports and, despite the apparent enthusiasm of Nicholas Ridley, this attitude persisted. At home Alan

Pegler was experiencing mounting financial difficulties, largely as a consequence of the continual drain that No 4472 was exerting on his funds and a rather high-profile divorce settlement.

However, within the States friendships established earlier in the tour began to bear fruit. An offer was made of initial funds and working capital from a group of US railfans, and there was a firm invitation to exhibit at British Week in San Francisco in 1972. A route was therefore planned with the cooperation of CN and Burlington Northern via Chicago to California. George Hinchcliffe again took advantage of his many friends and contacts to arrange stop-overs and source an excellent load of steam coal from the Peabody Coal Co in Joliet, Illinois. A volunteer was detailed to travel 24 hours ahead of the train, arranging local media coverage and publicity, and a volunteer crew was recruited to man the train.

On 19 August 1971 the locomotive was initially moved from the CN Spadina roundhouse alongside Toronto Union station to Bathurst to collect the exhibition cars, then on to Bronte in the Toronto western suburbs to collect the Pullman car *Lydia* and the Observation Car. The train was then moved by CN over the international bridge at Niagara Falls as far as Buffalo, New York, where a full week of preparation was required to ready the train for its 4,500-mile trip to San Francisco. Leaving Buffalo the train took the main Norfolk & Western (ex-New York, Chicago & St Louis 'Nickel Plate Road') route along the southern shore of Lake Erie through Cleveland and Fort Wayne to Blue Island yard in Chicago, before joining the former Rock Island tracks to Joliet. After taking on a new supply of coal at Joliet, the route was via the Elgin, Joliet & Eastern (EJE) to Aurora before joining the Burlington Northern's former CB&Q route forward via Savanna, Illinois, then following the Missouri River valley across Wisconsin to La Crosse and the twin cities of Minneapolis/St Paul. Thence the route was over the BN's former Great Northern main line across the Rockies through Minot, North Dakota, and Shelby, Montana, to Spokane in Washington State. Leaving Spokane on 12 September, the train continued on ex-GN tracks to Pasco before joining the BN's former Spokane, Portland & Seattle tracks to Wishram. After crossing into Oregon, the route was through Bend before rejoining former GN tracks proper on to Klamath Falls, entering California and heading on to Bieber. Southwards from Bieber the train was hosted by the Western Pacific Railroad, then joined the Feather River Canyon route at the famous Keddie 'Y' before reaching the destination of this leg at Oroville. Here the premises of a friend, Sam Girdlar, were used to refurbish the interior of the exhibition coaches before the train was worked down to Oakland. The crossing of San Francisco Bay direct to Fisherman's Wharf was undertaken in the traditional railroad manner – by barge (known in North America as a 'carfloat')!

Although the intention of the invitation to San Francisco was for the locomotive and train to be a starring, but static, attraction during British Week in 1972, this was too good an opportunity for the team to forego. The previously unprecedented operation of a passenger train along the San Francisco Belt Railroad did not happen without months of sometimes very delicate negotiations with a variety of different organisations. An initial approach in November 1971 brought forth a list of 45 requirements that would

have deterred most people made of less stern stuff than the Flying Scotsman Enterprises team. The requirements were prioritised and negotiations began, led by George Hinchcliffe. The key parties involved were the San Francisco Port Authority, the Belt Railroad, the Federal Railroad Administration, and representatives of the local Railroad Brotherhoods (the trades unions). Two days after the initial meeting, progress was immediately moved several stages forward when Henry Hilzinger, liaison officer with the FRA in Washington, arrived unheralded in San Francisco on holiday and immediately agreed to set up a meeting with all interested parties. With goodwill on all sides, agreement was soon reached sufficiently for the FRA to agree, subject to certain conditions, to a two-month experimental operation.

The executives of the Belt Railroad and their crews enthusiastically rose to the challenge to make technical changes to both the train and their tracks. Theory and practice were found to be at variance in a number of areas where trial movements demonstrated that the impossible was actually achievable. Compliance with FRA standards proved feasible in most areas, apart from the totally unfamiliar vacuum brake system. George made a detailed technical presentation supported by photocopies of the relevant pages of the BR *Handbook for Steam Locomotive Enginemen*. It was accepted that this was a fail-safe system and therefore met the FRA requirements but, not as George initially thought, as a result of his technical explanations, but because his audience totally failed to understand his presentation but accepted him as a credible witness!

The dockside section of the Belt Railroad chosen for the 2-mile-long shuttle operation ran from the tourist hot-spot of Fisherman's Wharf, where passengers joined the three-carriage train for the 70-minute round trip to Townsend Street and back, crossing many roadways, mostly without any traffic-light protection. The first day of operation was a test run with Belt Railroad and Port Authority officials on board, followed by a VIP special with local dignitaries, press, TV and radio. Extensive media coverage ensued and it became the 'in thing' in San Francisco to ride the *Flying Scotsman*. The first public day was 18 March 1971, when the Pacific Locomotive Association chartered the whole train for the day. The following day normal public services commenced, with passengers paying $3 for adults and $2 for children. During the operation along Fisherman's Wharf one particular visitor who happened to be on holiday with his wife was to prove very significant in the future of the locomotive, Sir William McAlpine. Bill McAlpine knew George Hinchcliffe and expressed anxiety about the future of the locomotive, asking to be kept informed and specifically contacted if No 4472's safety was in jeopardy.

Unfortunately the enthusiasm for the train apparent among the American public was not shared by the restaurant owners along Fisherman's Wharf. The loss of 92 car-parking spaces, which normally occupied the railroad tracks, was keenly felt, and pressure was soon applied to the authorities. As a result, after a few highly successful weeks of operation the train was moved further along Fisherman's Wharf to Powell Yard. Although only 100 yards along the Wharf, this move put the train so much out of the public eye that business quickly slumped by 90%.

Although initially the business plan targets had been achieved, to the extent that all debts would have been repaid inside 18 months, this collapse of takings had a disastrous impact on the project's finances. A review of the project against this background of a now bleak financial outlook prompted the decision to withdraw the train from service and take up the offer of storage at the Sharpe Army Base, south of Stockton, California. George Hinchcliffe arranged for the movement to be made on 14 August, wound up the business and returned to the UK.

The financial problems now became more pressing as the difficult position of the business became a matter of public speculation in the media, and creditors became ever more urgent in their demands for payment. Matters came to a head when Alan Pegler appeared in the London Bankruptcy Court on 31 October 1972. In January 1973 *The Railway Magazine* carried a report that the Transport Trust was involved in a campaign to return the locomotive to the UK, and in February reported that the Yorkshire Dales Railway was mounting a further rescue bid. Bill McAlpine had now became formally involved in a group led by Alan Bloom of Bressingham Museum, and George had a meeting with Alan Pegler, by now working as a cruise lecturer with P&O Cruises, on leave over Christmas 1972. Alan accepted that the rescue and transfer of ownership to Bill McAlpine was in the best long-term interests of the locomotive, and arrangements were hurriedly made for a party to travel to San Francisco early in the New Year in order to rescue it.

On 2 January 1973 George met with the group's American lawyer, who had already received urgent requests from the US railroads for payment of their outstanding accounts and were threatening to start legal proceedings. A final settlement of a little over half of the outstanding amounts was offered and, much to their surprise, was accepted. The Western Pacific Railroad agreed to move No 4472 from Sharpe Army Base to Oakland for a token sum, provided they never had to move No 4472 ever again! All that remained was to arrange shipment back to the UK. Here again fate played a part, as George had struck up a conversation with a fellow passenger during the flight to San Francisco who proved to work for a shipping line in San Francisco called Johnson Scanstar. Having explained his mission and exchanged contact numbers, George did not expect to hear from him again. However, shortly after returning from a meeting with his team of conspirators there was a message waiting: 'I have a ship sailing in 14 days, please phone.'

George now had a critical telephone conversation with Bill McAlpine in order to acquaint him with the latest estimate of costs to recover the locomotive and ship her back to the UK. The conversation ended with a request to George, 'If I buy the locomotive, will you run it?' Replying in the affirmative, George was told to go ahead and that the necessary funds would be made available. Initial plans were announced that No 4472 would, after repairs, be based at the new National Railway Museum at York. This was eventually to take place, but only after a further 32 years!

During the preparation of the locomotive for movement at the Sharpe Army Base, her supply of spares had to be evaluated, as not all could be returned to the UK. The supply of six spare driving springs was deemed essential and had to be transferred from the storage container for shipment in the locomotive tender. After failing to move the springs manually, assistance from a forklift truck was requested. Shortly afterwards a well-built US soldier appeared and amazed the group by easily manhandling the springs. An incredulous comment to the camp commander brought the response, 'Oh, so you have met Elmer then.' Elmer was the US Army weightlifting champion!

On Friday 19 January 1973, in conditions of some secrecy, as some creditors were as yet unpaid, three WP diesels moved the train of five box cars (for braking purposes) together with the locomotive, complete with her two tenders and a caboose, out of Sharpe Army Base over the Altamont Pass and through Niles Canyon and Fremont to Oakland, ready for shipment on the Blue Star Line cargo liner *California Star*. Curiously, Alan Pegler was in San Francisco at this time as lecturer on board the P&O liner *Canberra* and was able to meet up with George. The hope was that, with the intervening weekend, the movement would attract little attention and the locomotive would be at sea before anybody noticed. Unfortunately the movement of the floating crane across San Francisco Bay created some interest from a local reporter, but he was successfully intercepted and persuaded, by being liberally supplied with Scotch whisky, to hold filing his story until the ship was outside US territorial waters. This was highly critical as one of the outstanding creditors was the San Francisco Port Authority!

Thus in mid-January 1972 the ship slipped her moorings and set sail for Panama via Los Angeles. The mv *California Star* was a British-flagged cargo liner of 19,095grt, built in 1971 and operating a regular service from US West Coast ports via the Panama Canal to Liverpool. No 4472 and her two tenders were secured as deck cargo flanked by a protective screen of containers. On arrival in Liverpool on 13 February 1973, No 4472 was unloaded in Huskisson Dock by *Mammoth*, the same MDHB floating crane that had loaded her some 3½ years earlier.

No 4472 arrives at Eisenhower's birthplace, Denison, Texas, on 20 June 1970.
*Emery J. Gulash*

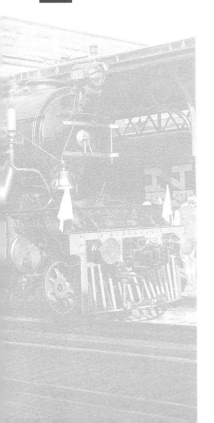

Once unloaded on to British soil again, No 4472 was moved to Edge Hill shed and inspected by BR engineers and pronounced fit to steam. However, at this time steam locomotives were not exactly highly regarded by BR and a decree was issued from on high that the locomotive was to be diesel-hauled to Derby Works for repairs. Fortunately the BR Divisional Manager in Liverpool at this time was noted steam enthusiast Richard Hardy, and he refused to allow one of his diesel locomotives to be used for the movement as it might get 'lost' and fail to be promptly returned to Liverpool. The faithful GMRS band were reassembled and made a successful attempt to smarten up No 4472, removing the ravages of the Atlantic crossing. A willing crew was found, and *Flying Scotsman* had steam raised for the first time in almost two years, ready to depart on 19 February under her own steam to Derby via Manchester and the Hope Valley line. This was a high-profile media event and throughout her journey crowds gathered at the lineside, including a group of schoolchildren carrying a banner proclaiming 'Welcome Home Scottie'.

During the series of 'Cider Express' specials featuring the Bulmer's Pullman carriages, No 4472 poses on 7 October 1973 at Tyseley, alongside the 15-inch-gauge Romney, Hythe & Dymchurch Railway 'Pacific' No 3 *Southern Maid*. Five of these locomotives were built using original 'A1' class drawings loaned by Nigel Gresley to Davey Paxman of Colchester in 1925/6. *Millbrook House*

Some repairs were necessary before BR was satisfied that No 4472 could join the limited number of steam locomotives permitted to run over its lines, Alan Pegler's running agreement having expired in 1971. However, the Paignton to Kingswear branch had recently been acquired as a tourist steam line by the Dart Valley Railway, which decided that a summer visit by No 4472 was just the publicity boost that their new venture required. Accordingly a contract was agreed that saw No 4472, together with Bill McAlpine's ex-Caledonian Saloon No 41 and Saloon No GE1, leave Derby on 14 July 1973 for Paignton so that No 4472 could spend the entire summer timetable period working trains between Paignton and Kingswear. After this, on 22 September, No 4472

In March 1974 No 4472 is stabled at her temporary home at Market Overton. Note the second tender, yet to be commissioned. *Mike Dobson*

made a triumphant return to the main line working the 15-coach Newport to Shrewsbury 'Atlantic Venturers Express', double-headed with No 6000 *King George V*, which had also visited the USA some 40 years earlier. A close association was now forged with Bulmer's and the 6000 Locomotive Association, which saw No 4472 take the five Bulmer's Pullman cars attached at Newport forward from Shrewsbury on a tour of the North of England, promoting Bulmer's products. The tour commenced

at Manchester Victoria station on 24 September and visited Sheffield, York, Newcastle and Carlisle, finishing on 3 October. During the course of the return journey No 4472 was worked up to 96mph. The locomotive and train then returned to Hereford via the Tyseley Open Day on 7 October.

A permanent home for No 4472 was now urgently required. Bill McAlpine and John (now Lord) Gretton had established a steam centre at the British Steel iron ore mining complex at Market Overton in Lincolnshire, with main-line access at High Dyke, 4 miles south of Grantham. Thus for the winter of 1973/74 No 4472 joined a number of preserved industrial steam locomotives and her former GWR 'Castle' class companion at the Wembley Exhibition in 1924/25, No 4079 *Pendennis Castle*. On 29 March 1974 the two locomotives left Market Overton, No 4079 heading direct to Hereford and No 4472 heading initially to Bletchley for Bletchley Urban District Council on 30 March. By 6 April No 4472 had returned to the Welsh Marches to work two trains from Newport to Shrewsbury and back jointly with *Pendennis Castle*. These trips with identical loads over the same route provided the opportunity for an interesting comparison between the relative performances of the two old rivals. No 4472, despite the weight of her second tender, proved to be by far the most economical locomotive, burning some 3 tons less coal than No 4079. After the ignominy of the 1923 Locomotive Exchanges, the honour of Gresley was definitely restored. This was followed by a month's visit to the Dinting Railway Centre at Glossop in Derbyshire in late April and early May.

Unfortunately changes in the steel industry saw a move away from low-grade domestic iron ore in favour of imports, and the Colsterworth mine complex was forced to close in 1974. This meant that the Market Overton depot was to lose its main-line connection on 12 November and was therefore doomed to close. For the 1975 Motor Show at London's Olympia, the Wakefield Castrol Oil Company had hired No 4472 to be a feature on its stand, so a movement to London was required. Also, in 1974 plans had emerged for a celebration of the 150th anniversary of the opening of the Stockton & Darlington Railway, to be held in August

1975. No 4472 was obviously going to be invited to attend, and this, combined with the problems at Market Overton, caused a search for a new home.

George Hinchcliffe took the practical view that a base close to one of the new regular steam routes was a highly desirable condition, and discussions with Joe Greenwood and Peter Beet, who had set up the steam centre at the former Carnforth loco shed in Lancashire, brought forth an investment by Bill McAlpine that saw George installed as Managing Director of Flying Scotsman Enterprises Steamtown Carnforth. *Flying Scotsman* was moved direct from the Motor Show to Carnforth, and the remaining rolling stock from Market Overton, including *Pendennis Castle*, was moved across to join No 4472, arriving on 14 November 1974. Meanwhile No 4472 had commenced operations from her new Carnforth home on 21 September, running with No 4771 *Green Arrow* on two special trains from Carnforth to Sellafield, with the locomotives exchanging trains for the return journey. This was followed on 29 September by a return trip from York to Scarborough for the 'Northern Gas Newcastle Festival Special'.

The highlight of 1975 was the 'Stockton & Darlington 150' celebrations. On 31 August No 4472 hauls ex-NER Fletcher 2-4-0 No 901 of 1872 during the cavalcade. *G. R. Hounsell*

The big event of 1975 was the 'S&D 150' celebration and exhibition, which was to culminate in a grand cavalcade to be held at Shildon on 31 August. Before then further trips were run on 21 June to Sellafield, again working two trains jointly with *Green Arrow*. The movement to Shildon took place on 17 August, with a most unusual train departing from Carnforth for Leeds and York. No 4472 was hauling the ex-Caledonian saloon No 41, but as pilot to *Flying Scotsman* was the LNWR victor of the 1899 'Race to the North', veteran 2-4-0 No 790 *Hardwicke*. The latter had been restored to steam at Carnforth by a small team, and those honoured to ride on the footplate of No 4472 recall that, looking forward, the diminutive No 790 was almost invisible.

The Cavalcade at Shildon was designed to be as historically accurate as possible, so non-steamable exhibits were paired with the most appropriate partner. No 4472 hauled the ancient NER Fletcher 2-4-0, and No 4498 *Sir Nigel Gresley* was given the task of hauling the GNR Stirling 4-2-2 No 1. As a follow-up to 'S&D 150' a series of steam-hauled special trains was run from Sheffield to Newcastle and back on Sundays in September. No 4472 participated in these with Nos 4498, 4771 and 'B1' 1306 *Mayflower*. On 21 September a combination of circumstances after the failure of No 4771 saw a 15-coach train worked by No 4472, double-heading with No 1306 from York to Newcastle and back to Sheffield.

No 4472 has always been a favourite backdrop for film producers, and one instance that took place in 1975 is worth relating. The feature film *Agatha*, starring Dustin Hoffman and Vanessa Redgrave, was shooting scenes at York station, disguised as Harrogate. No 4472 appeared in several shots as variously No 4474 *Victor Wild* and No 4480 *Enterprise*, hauling an assortment of Pullman cars. After the shooting was finished No 4472 hauled a motley collection of vehicles, including SR 4-6-0 No 850 *Lord Nelson* and the 1908 Bletchley breakdown train from York back to Carnforth.

Early in 1976 an agreement was announced between the National Railway Museum, Steamtown Carnforth, Flying Scotsman Enterprises and British Rail

In May 1976 No 4472 has an unusual pilot in the form of ex-LNWR 2-4-0 No 790 *Hardwicke* as she leaves Carnforth for Grange-over-Sands. *G. A. Richardson*

for an exchange of locomotives. No 4472 was to be exchanged for both No 1000, the Midland Compound, and the ex-LNWR 2-4-0 No 790 *Hardwicke*. The change-over trips took place on 24 April and the return workings were arranged for 19 June. Between these dates many strange combinations took to the main line – mostly as a result of No 1000's prompt failure on arrival at Carnforth.

One early example was a special run to celebrate the centenary of the Settle & Carlisle line on 1 May.

Neither of the intended combination of No 1000 and 'Black Five' No 44932 was available, so the train was hauled by No 4472, piloted by No 790. An identical formation was turned out on 22 May between Carnforth and Ulverston.

Throughout 1977 No 4472 continued to work occasional trips from her Carnforth base, including on 17 September a special for the LNER Society that utilised not only No 4472 but also the newly overhauled No 4771 *Green Arrow* and No 4498

*Sir Nigel Gresley*, all working separate sections of a Carnforth-Leeds-York-Leeds-Carnforth route.

By the end of 1977 some four years of work had been undertaken and the need for a further overhaul had been identified. This time it was to be Vickers Armstrong's Barrow-in-Furness shipyard that was to undertake the work, which included an exchange of boilers. During the six-month overhaul, boiler No 27971 from 'A4' No 60019 *Bittern* was fitted. The fitting of an 'A4' boiler was not unprecedented as the two boilers were similar and several 'A3s' had carried 'A4' boilers towards the end of their lives. Boiler No 27020 became a spare, retained for possible future use.

On 6 June 1978 No 4472 emerged from Vickers works and promptly re-entered main-line service with a press preview of the new 'Cumbrian Coast Express' ('CCE') service operating between Carnforth and Sellafield. Two days later No 4472 worked a special formed of privately owned vintage coaches from Hellifield to Carlisle, returning on 9 June. The regular 'CCE' service operated on Tuesdays and Wednesdays, 27 June to 29 August,

the train originating at Blackpool with diesel haulage to Preston and Carnforth before a change to steam traction for the journey to Sellafield. The 19 trains operated by either No 4472 or No 4498 carried 9,230 passengers.

A rather sad event had taken place on 13 May when the noted railway photographer the Rt Rev Bishop Eric Treacy died at Appleby station while waiting to photograph No 92220 *Evening Star*. In a highly poignant tribute on 30 September, two trains named 'The Lord Bishop' and 'Bishop Treacy' were operated by three locomotives, Nos 92220, 35028 *Clan Line* and 4472 over the Settle & Carlisle line, with a commemorative service taking place in the station yard at Appleby.

In a new venture on 30 December the 'CCE' format was amended to be a 13-coach 'Santa Steam Special' from Euston to Sellafield, hauled from Carnforth by No 4472.

In 1979 the 'Cumbrian Coast Express' operated on Tuesdays and Thursdays between May and September, with a new 'North Yorkshireman' train operating on Wednesdays between Grange-over-

On 30 December 1978 No 4472 catches the last rays of the setting winter sun as she returns a 'Cumbrian Coast Express' New Year special across the River Mite Viaduct at Ravenglass. *R. Peachey*

On 8 August 1979 No 4472 heads the outwards 'North Yorkshireman' past Giggleswick en route to Skipton. *J. H. Cooper-Smith*

On 4 July 1979 No 4472 shares the coaling plant at Carnforth with No 35028 *Clan Line*, which had recently arrived with the 'North Yorkshireman' from Keighley. *W. A. Sharman*

Sands and Skipton. No 4472 was part of a pool of four locomotives working these trains, being joined at Carnforth by Nos 4498, 35028 and 5690 *Leander*. That year was also the centenary of rail catering, and an exhibition train composed of vintage catering vehicles toured the country, being hauled over the Settle & Carlisle line by No 4472. The year ended with another 'Santa Steam Special' to Ravenglass on 30 December.

The following year, 1980, began with a visit during 19/20 February to the Worth Valley Railway at Keighley for the filming of a television advertisement for Hovis bread. On 12 March No 4472 hauled a special Post Office train between Liverpool and Manchester for the 'Mail 150' first day issue of a set of Rail 150 stamps.

The high point of 1980 was undoubtedly the Whitsun weekend celebrations of the 150th anniversary of the opening of the Liverpool & Manchester Railway, 'Rocket 150', in which No 4472 took a prominent part.

In conjunction with the filming of an episode of the BBC's *Great Railway Journeys of the World*' on 15 June, No 4472 worked a 195-mile special throughout from Guide Bridge to Carnforth via York. In addition she worked 12 separate 'Cumbrian Mountain Express' ('CME') trains over the Settle & Carlisle line. Further 'Santa Special' workings ended off the year, with No 4472 again working from Sellafield to Carnforth on 27 December.

Filming at Keighley on 20 February 1980 required No 4472 to visit Haworth for servicing and here, just after dawn, she returns to Keighley, passing through the delightful Oakworth station, made famous as Mr Perks's station in *The Railway Children*.
*R. Greenwood, K&WVR*

There is still snow on the fell tops as No 4472 enters Birkett Tunnel with the up 'Cumbrian Mountain Express' on 5 April 1980. *L. A. Nixon*

With a misty Pen-y-Ghent in the background, No 4472 hauls a northbound 'Cumbrian Mountain Express' off Ribblehead Viaduct on 12 April 1980. *W. A. Sharman*

In 1981 No 4472 carried on from the previous year's pattern between May and September, sharing in working the 'CCE' on Tuesdays, the 'CME' on Wednesdays and a revised 'North Yorkshireman' on Thursdays. This now featured a Carnforth to Keighley itinerary, with the stock being serviced at Bradford while the locomotive turned at Shipley.

One significant happening in 1982 was a first encounter with Roland Kennington, when he joined the No 4498 support crew, working alongside No 4472 at Carnforth. Roland was later to become the engineer responsible for No 4472 for almost 20 years between 1985 and 2004. No 4472's summer work continued the pattern of Tuesday 'CMEs', but Wednesday's 'CCE' was extended to Maryport on alternate days, the other day seeing a new Carnforth to York train designed to facilitate the movement of locomotives between bases. In the midst of this regular pattern No 4472 worked two school specials over the Settle & Carlisle line, first a Langwathby to York and return train on 1 July, then working the next day from Carlisle to York and back, positioning the locomotive for a

No 4472 leaves Skipton for Carnforth with a Guide Bridge to Carnforth special in connection with a BBC *Great Railway Journeys* filming on 15 June 1980. *W. A. Sharman*

southbound 'CME' on 20 July. On the 21st No 4472 worked a Carnforth to York 'White Rose', and on the following day the inaugural 'Scarborough Spa Express' of the season.

The year 1983 was a very special one for No 4472, being her Diamond Jubilee. Plans had begun to be formulated in the summer of 1982, with an initial BR suggestion of a Preston to Leeds trip. George Hinchcliffe was anxious to get No 4472 back on to her old East Coast hunting ground, and a chance holiday visit to Steamtown by the then BR Director Inter-City, Cyril Bleasdale, known to George from when he had been Area Manager at Doncaster during No 4472's sojourn there in the 1960s, presented a not-to-be-missed opportunity. Plans were developed for the Leeds trip to be extended to York for an NRM visit before a Grantham to York run. This was later changed to Peterborough as operationally more convenient. Actually falling on 27 February, the Diamond Jubilee was celebrated on the 24th in a ceremony at Steamtown Carnforth, followed by No 4472 hauling the special train to Leeds. Unfortunately a

load of cheap domestic coal had been purchased in error and this caused significant steaming problems on the outward journey. This train was a positioning run for what became a series of three sell-out Peterborough to York Diamond Jubilee specials operated on 27 February, 6 and 13 March. Fortunately fresh supplies of good Yorkshire coal were obtained and No 4472 put up some sparking performances. One oddity during these trips was that No 4472 actually ran with the tender from No 4498, suitably repainted, as her own tender was out of service under repair.

After sharing in the usual summer programme of 'CME' and 'CCE' trains, No 4472 broke new ground in October 1983 when on the 22nd she worked a train from Annan to Ayr before being the star attraction at the Ayr Rail Fair on the 29th and 30th. Return south was made on 12 November with an Ayr to Carlisle train. Further East Coast work followed, with a requirement to work an exhibition train for Sir Robert McAlpine & Sons calling at Newcastle, Edinburgh and Glasgow. During the return journey between Darlington and

York, when hauling the Bulmer's Pullmans and Saloon No GE1, both the Inspector and driver were working their last trip before retirement. The speedometer was noted at one stage displaying 96mph and the Northallerton to York section took less than 26 minutes for the 30 miles.

The highlight of 1984 was to be the November visit to the opening of the East London Museum at North Woolwich by HM the Queen Mother. But first there was a need to participate in the usual programme of 'CME', 'CCE' and 'Scarborough Spa Express' trains, beginning as early as 25 February with a 'Cumbrian Mountain Express' to Carlisle. During a very hot summer several instances of lineside fires caused cancellations, and No 4472 gained a new spark arrester for a 19 July 'CME' trip. On 22 September there was a promotional trip from Manchester Victoria to Chester via Northwich

In a first appearance on the East Coast Main Line since 1969, on 27 February 1983 No 4472 storms up the last section of Stoke bank with the first of three sold-out King's Cross to Scarborough trains, which she worked from Peterborough. *D. Percival*

on behalf of Wilson's Brewery. The movement to North Woolwich began on 10 November with a 'Fenman' Manchester Victoria to Spalding trip ready for the Royal Train from Stratford (Low Level) to North Woolwich on 20 November, returning north from Spalding to Manchester on the 24th.

Most of 1985 was spent at Steamtown undergoing a general overhaul, it being seven years since the previous 1978 overhaul at Vickers. That the locomotive managed to achieve the full seven years' use from her main-line 'ticket' was a reflection on the quality of the care lavished on her by the staff at Steamtown and the financial generosity of her owner Bill McAlpine. During this period Roland Kennington became involved with the support team at Carnforth and eventually took over as No 4472's Chief Engineer from May 1986. With a new seven-year 'ticket' issued on 27 November 1985, No 4472 moved south on 27 December to Marylebone in order to participate in the new highly successful 'Shakespeare Express' Sunday lunch trains. The first train to be worked by No 4472 was two days later on 29 December.

The following year began with a special occasion, a private 'Shakespeare Express' from Marylebone on 12 January 1986 to celebrate Bill McAlpine's 50th birthday. The BR-sponsored 'Shakespeare Express' Sunday lunch trains continued to prosper, being worked by a pool of four locos, Nos 4472 *Flying Scotsman*, 4498 *Sir Nigel Gresley*, 777 *Sir Lamiel* and 35028 *Clan Line*. Unfortunately, despite the long overhaul the previous year at Carnforth, No 4472 experienced a number of persistent mechanical failures culminating on 5 May with problems on a return 'Shakespeare' at High Wycombe, which caused temporary withdrawal until a successful test run to Banbury on 14 September. Difficulties in effecting repairs at the temporary base in the BR diesel depot at Marylebone brought about a rethink in maintenance strategy, with the decision by Bill McAlpine to lease the two-road former diesel maintenance shop at Southall. This gave the London area a new base for main-line steam operations with room for up to eight locomotives, illuminated inspection pits, a small workshop and other useful facilities.

The suitability of the depot had been demonstrated earlier in 1986 when it had been used for an extensive overhaul by No 35028 *Clan Line*. Negotiations were concluded in December for a one-to-three-year lease to Flying Scotsman Enterprises, and thus Southall became No 4472's new home base. Despite this relocation No 4472 continued to work trains out of Marylebone, culminating on 28 December with a 'Santa Special' to Stratford.

That year also brought forward a proposal for an interesting new fortnightly summer service to be worked by No 4472, from Derby to Matlock, for a visit to Chatsworth House. Unfortunately this never really got off the ground and No 4472 continued to participate in the weekly Stratford-upon-Avon trips from Marylebone. A problem at High Wycombe on a returning 'Shakespeare Express' in June caused by a lubrication failure required a nine-week intensive period of attention overhauling all the major cylinder and motion components and valve setting by the former Norwich shedmaster Bill Harvey. For Bill this was the renewal of an acquaintance with No 4472

that had begun in 1924 when, as an apprentice at Doncaster Works, he had worked on preparing the locomotive for her exhibition at Wembley. An initial test run to High Wycombe was unsuccessful but,

No 4472 sits in the platform at Marylebone prior to working the 'Shakespeare Limited' service to Stratford on Avon on 12 October 1986. Note the polished quartered buffers. *D. Percival*

after a further fortnight's work, a fortunately uneventful trip on 14 September led to the locomotive being pronounced fit for further work, re-entering service with the 28 September 'Shakespeare'. An innovation for Christmas 1986 was a series of Marylebone to High Wycombe 'Santa Special' trains. For the Saturday and Sunday of the two weekends prior to Christmas two trips were run each day utilising Nos 4472, 35028 and 777. These trains all sold out well before the due dates and were therefore replicated on the first weekend in January 1987. Again the 28 December Stratford train, hauled by No 4472, was so popular that it had to be duplicated. This train also marked the first appearance on a steam charter of one of the 'ETHEL' converted diesel locomotives, required in order to provide train-heating as facilities to maintain steam-heated rolling stock were no longer available.

The first 'Shakespeare Express' of 1987 ran on 18 January, with a further ten trains planned in the period up to the end of June. The change this year was termination of the steam haulage at Banbury, supposedly to facilitate locomotive turning, which was still undertaken on the triangle at Hatton. Unfortunately No 4472 was failed on 15 February with a fractured lubricator pipe to the middle cylinder and the train had to be diesel-hauled, despite the standby loco No 777 being lit up and then herself failing with a separate lubrication problem. The failure of No 4498 with a tender wheelset problem reduced the Marylebone pool to only three locomotives, so plans were made for No 4771 *Green Arrow* to work south from York on 21 March. No 4771 was not ready in time, so No 4472 worked a replacement trip from Marylebone to Sheffield and back. The next day No 4472 worked to Banbury and back, encompassing 607 miles in two days' running. A series of 'Sellafield Sightseer' trains were sponsored by BNFL in the spring of 1987 with No 4472 as the requested power, so she worked a 293-mile trip from Marylebone to Carnforth on 5 April in order to regain her old home at Carnforth. During April, May and June she worked five separate 'Sellafield Sightseer' trains which, from 25 May, she was able to work in both directions after the commissioning of the turning triangle at Sellafield.

In between these trips No 4472 made a visit to the BR Coalville Open Day on 30 May 1987 after being used by Cromwell Tools to work a series of promotional 'Cromwell Pullman' trips between Leicester and Dorridge between 1 and 5 May. June saw a visit to Salisbury for three weekends of running to and from Yeovil, during which the locomotive ran 2,062 miles. After returning to Marylebone the motion was dismantled to facilitate a movement to Ilford depot for the driving wheels to have their tyres reprofiled on 23 June. July and August saw three 'Scarborough Spa Express' trains worked, which included a derailment of the Cartazzi truck at York after the first trip on 26 July. The subsequent detailed examination revealed that an error in the measuring system at Ilford had led to the wheels being machined to different sizes. A visit to the wheel lathe at Thornaby depot restored normality, but now at least two wheels were at scrapping size. On 23 August No 4472 undertook a promotional trip from Manchester to Chester for Halls Mentholyptus. After working a private Sellafield trip for Bill McAlpine on 15 October, on return to Carnforth No 4472 was found to have damaged white metal in the axleboxes of two axles. As this was thought to be caused by the formerly irregular tyre sizes, the locomotive was withdrawn from service pending the fitting of new driving wheel tyres.

In anticipation of this work, and in the light of the developing plans for the forthcoming Australian visit, axlebox repairs were undertaken and successfully run-in on some 'Mince-Pie Specials' at Carnforth over Christmas 1987. Revised plans were now made for the locomotive to be worked south to Southall, where the wheeldrop would facilitate removal of the driving wheelsets for tyre replacement by Doncaster Works. Thus No 4472 returned south at the head of a 'Lancastrian' charter on 27 February 1988, again working the 275 miles from Carnforth to West Ruislip. In the 16 months since the High Wycombe test run the locomotive had run 10,917 miles without failure. The driving wheels were removed at Southall the very next day, 28 February, and immediately sent off to Doncaster for the fitting of new tyres, completion being due by late April. In the event it was 15 July before the newly retired wheelsets returned to Southall. During this period major mechanical repairs were also completed, and it took until 11 August before No 4472 was ready to make a test run to Tyseley, returning from Banbury to Marylebone with a 'Shakespeare Express' on the 14th. Following completion of final painting and lining, the locomotive emerged for photographs on 2 September, leaving eight days for final adjustments and loading of spares in readiness for the final movement to Tilbury in preparation for embarkation for Australia.

On 16 May 1987 No 4472, posed in front of the coaling tower at Carnforth, shares the limelight with newly arrived No 4468 *Mallard*. *J. B. Gosling, Millbrook House*

The Australian Bicentennial was to take place in 1988, and in anticipation of this milestone a group of Australian enthusiasts had formed an 'Aus Steam '88' committee, to ensure that the pivotal role of railways in the story of Australia was not to be overlooked and that suitable celebrations were to be held. The Chairman of 'Aus Steam '88', Walter Stuchbery, who was to play a pivotal role in the planning and execution of the celebrations, had approached the UK National Railway Museum in 1987 to ascertain the availability of No 4468 *Mallard*. Although *Mallard* was put back into steam in 1985, this was done to a very limited budget and was subject to a severe limit on the number of occasions on which the locomotive could be steamed. Invitations had already been received from France and The Netherlands, which had all had to be refused, as there was no funding available for the further boiler repairs that would have been required for any extension to the boiler certificate. It was Dr Coiley, Head of the NRM, who suggested to Walter Stuchbery that he contact Sir William McAlpine with a view to inviting No 4472 *Flying Scotsman* in *Mallard*'s place.

Thus it was that in early 1988 George Hinchcliffe was dispatched to Australia to discuss detailed arrangements for the visit of No 4472. Plans were confirmed for the locomotive to run almost 20,000 miles and visit at least four of the mainland states, Tasmania's narrow gauge preventing any visit to that island, during a six-month visit from the autumn of 1988 to the spring of 1989.

On 11 September 1988 No 4472 was loaded by the PLA floating crane *London Samson* on the deck of the P&O Line container ship *New Zealand Pacific*. This Hong Kong-flagged vessel, built in 1978 of 43,704nrt, sailed from Tilbury on the 14th and arrived at Sydney after a 32-day passage on 16 October, sailing via the Mediterranean, the Suez Canal and the Indian Ocean. At Sydney the Cockatoo Dockyard's floating crane *Titan* was used to unload the locomotive and tender at Wharf 13, Pyrmont, Sydney Harbour. The locomotive was quickly moved to the NSW State Rail Authority depot at Eveleigh in preparation for a test run on 18 October south from Sydney to Waterfall. This was successfully accomplished and an NSW

certification of the locomotive was obtained. One of the key concerns of the NSW Rail Authority had been the ability of No 4472 to haul a 300-ton load unassisted up the 1 in 34 Cowan Bank on the line north to Gosford. George had reassured the authorities that this was well within No 4472's capabilities and fortunately the locomotive proved George's confidence to be well placed.

The first movement of No 4472, after the test run to Waterfall, was an unadvertised positioning movement over the 596-mile route through to Melbourne, Victoria, where the 'Aus Steam '88' Open Day at the Spencer Street station awaited. Despite the low-key nature of this movement, huge crowds turned out to see the train pass the numerous level crossings and pace the train along the adjacent Hume Highway. On the first day the scene was set when the servicing stop at the small town of Goulburn, 141 miles south of Sydney, saw a crowd of more than 300 enthusiasts turn out to see the train. Then, having passed from New South Wales into Victoria at Albury, the first town of any size was Wangaratta. Here the crowds were so large that the train had to slow to walking pace and the northbound 'Intercapital Daylight Express' was stopped, its tracks blocked by spectators.

The crowd on arrival at Spencer Street station in Melbourne on 25 October was estimated at 130,000 people. Although Victoria, being a broad gauge state, could only offer trips over the 1962-built 191-mile standard gauge North Eastern main line between Melbourne and Albury, one particular feature of the runs in Victoria was the rather cavalier way in which the official speed limit of 50mph was widely disregarded, with speeds of 88mph and 84mph (twice) being recorded.

As the 'Standard Gauge State', New South Wales was to see more of No 4472 than any other part of Australia. The formal welcome to New South Wales was held in the Southern Highlands at Moss Vale, 89 miles out of Sydney, on 18 December, during the course of a Melbourne to Sydney movement that had commenced the previous day. Here a crowd of 5,000 had gathered to see the 'meet' between No 4472 and the official bicentennial locomotive, 'C38' class 'Pacific' No 3801. Also present was Baldwin-built 'D59' class 2-8-2 No 5910, splendidly turned out by the New South Wales Transport Museum at Thirlmere. Later in the day, hauling her own train, No 4472 was to run the 56 miles from Gosford to Sydney's Central station in a parallel movement alongside No 3801, hauling the Bicentennial carriage set.

After a rest over the Christmas period, the tour recommenced in January 1989. A six-week series of trips were run from Sydney, with three trips being run on Saturdays and Sundays over either the 56 miles to Gosford, the 51 miles to Wollongong or the 99 miles to Lithgow. But first, on 30 January was a special 112-mile Dynamometer Car round trip over the Main North line to Gosford and back. On the return this involved an unassisted climb up the 1 in 34 Cowan Bank, which was achieved in some style.

Next came a visit to Queensland, which began on 24 March. The train formation was a substantial 12 cars for the four-day 687-mile trip to Brisbane. With a train of this size assistance was essential, and 'C38' 4-6-2 No 3801 was utilised to assist No 4472 throughout. In almost all trips in Australia

In August 1989 No 4472 departs Spencer Street station in Melbourne alongside broad gauge North British-built 'Hudson' 4-6-4 No 707. *Graham Withers*

No 4472 was coupled at the front of the train. This had been agreed with the Australian railway authorities on the basis that No 4472's front bufferbeam was insufficiently strong to carry the stresses of another locomotive coupled in front. This entirely erroneous belief had been fostered by the *Flying Scotsman* team with the clear aspiration that No 4472 would always lead! Day one took the train 120 miles along the magnificently scenic Hawkesbury River and Central Coast towns before swinging inland to Maitland. Day two was a 193-mile leg off the Great Northern line to attack the mountainous grades and winding route to the North Coast and Kempsey. The next day was towards the forbidding McPherson Ranges, then entering Queensland through the famous border loop. Here the train circumnavigates a mountain by crossing over itself twice, then passes through a tunnel before emerging in Queensland. After ten days on exhibition at Roma Street station in Brisbane, and after working a 95-mile day trip to Kyogle, the train returned south to Sydney. The next event was on 18 April, a Steam Festival back at Maitland, where No 4472 again shared the limelight with more parallel running alongside No 3801.

Next was a recreation of the famous 'Western Mail' train over the 262 miles from Sydney to Dubbo on Friday 9 June. Again No 4472 was paired with No 3801 for the long overnight journey. The first leg was 34 miles to the foothills of the Blue Mountains at Penrith. A little further on, at Valley Heights, a brief stop was required to attach a third locomotive, 4-6-4 tank No 3112, for assistance over the steepest grades as far as milepost 68 at Katoomba. As the clock ticked past midnight into Saturday, the train passed over the Darling Causeway Bridge, at 3,350 feet above sea level the highest railway point between the Pacific and Indian Oceans. The descent to Lithgow was through the ten tunnels opened in 1910 to replace the awesome Great Zig Zag, built in the 1860s to get trains down from the Blue Mountains to the Western Plains beyond.

Then it was through Bathurst and Orange, before leaving the East-West 'Indian Pacific' route and branching north to Wellington and Dubbo. Further trips were run out of Sydney throughout June and July, including a return visit to Lithgow on 25 June, before a return to Melbourne at the end of July. This was to allow preparation for the most ambitious part of the tour, the crossing of the continent.

Thus it was that No 4472 stood serviced and ready at Melbourne's Spencer Street station on 6 August 1989 ready to depart for the eight-day trip to the heart of the continent at Alice Springs. The route was back to Albury and the Murray River for the last time, thence via the New South Wales southern trunk route through Wagga Wagga to Cootamundra. But first there was to be the spectacular sight of three steam-hauled trains running in parallel over the 62 miles between Melbourne and Seymour. No 4472 was run on the right-hand (easterly) standard gauge track with broad gauge 'R' class 4-6-4 No 761 and sister locomotive No 707 pacing alongside on the twin broad gauge tracks. Onwards from Cootamundra, the route diverted across the NSW wheat belt to join the main east-west route at Parkes.

The scene was thus set on 8 August for another of No 4472's world record runs. It had become the practice in Australia to make much longer runs between water stops than is usual in the UK, usually with the assistance of water tank wagons to supplement the tender supply. Roland Kennington thought that this offered the opportunity to establish a new world record non-stop run, and the 422-mile section from Parkes to Broken Hill seemed to offer the best opportunity for this. It required careful planning and the full cooperation of the NSW State Rail Authority, as the two crews would be required to cooperate and every one of the passing loops would have to be staffed. Normally only four of the 14 token-exchange points were manned, requiring trains to stop at the other ten to carry out safety procedures. For one day only the NSW authorities agreed to man all crossing points so that the non-stop attempt could be mounted.

The train was composed of eight passenger cars and no fewer than three 'water gin' cars, totalling 465 tons. The 422-mile trip took 9hr 25min and was only successful because of two separate items of good luck. First, two paths had been offered from Maitland, departing at 5.00am or 8.00am. Fortunately they opted for the former, as this offered a less busy run with fewer trains about, and the passengers also agreed the early start. If the later path had been taken they would have been delayed by the later failure of the Broken Hill to Orange 'Silver City Comet'. In addition, about halfway along the route at Ivanhoe, tired fingers dropped the single-line staff, but it was recovered by a support crew member before the train was stopped at the Home signal. The previous record was 408 miles, established in 1948 when the 'Flying Scotsman' train had been diverted via St Boswells because of flood damage to bridges on the usual route.

After the record-breaking run, and before arriving in the Silver City of Broken Hill, the next section was a canter over the rolling plains into South Australia and Port Augusta. As the stark beauty of the Flinders Range faded into the distance, No 4472 had now acquired extra insurance in the form of a GM diesel, two crew cars and a generator car, adding up to a train of 735 tons. The next stop was Tarcoola, where No 4472 rattled over the junction and became the first steam locomotive to traverse the 1980-built 490-mile standard gauge line to Alice Springs. Later in the afternoon of 14 August No 4472 and her huge train slipped through the McPherson Gap in the McDonald Ranges and entered Alice Springs. This was after a most unusual meet at Lubcke Siding, just outside Alice, the only place where the old 3ft 6in 'Old Ghan' line parallels the new standard gauge route; here a greeting was exchanged with the preserved narrow gauge 'W' class 4-8-2 No W924 running alongside No 4472 and her train. The train then returned to Tarcoola for the next stage of the run to Western Australia. Private sponsors had been found, NSW coaches rustled up and Australian National diesels pressed into service to assist No 4472 for the 1,198 miles across the Nullarbor Plain to Perth. This included traversing the 299 miles of the longest dead level and straight piece of line in the world.

Over the last section of the route into Perth, No 4472 had assistance from another steam locomotive – no stranger this time, but an old friend from Wembley, Hereford and Market Overton, No 4079 *Pendennis Castle*. Since 1978 No 4079 had been resident on the Hammersley Iron Company's isolated ore-carrying line at Parraburdoo in Western Australia. The opportunity for the two locomotives to meet up was too great to resist, so arrangements were made to transport No 4079 to Perth. Again the Australian gauge diversity was to prevent any extensive running in Western Australia as, apart from the single transcontinental line into Perth, all of the Western Australia network is composed of 3ft 6in gauge lines. During September several trips were run out of Perth, many double-heading with No 4079, but in Sydney there was a date to be kept with a boat for England. No 4472 returned east to be met again by No 3801 for the last stage from Orange to Sydney.

The final public journey in Australia was on 29 October 1989. This was a trip from Darling Harbour, in central Sydney, to Gosford, up the Main North line on the Central Coast. This presented the final challenge of yet another assault on the return journey of the infamous 1 in 34 Cowan Bank, achieved in style with assistance from the ever-faithful No 3801. In 55 weeks No 4472 had run 28,000 miles, without any major mechanical problems in an excellent tribute to the quality of the overhaul undertaken at Southall in 1988 by Roland Kennington and his team.

Again the floating crane *Titan* was used to load No 4472 at Sydney's No 13 Wharf at Pyrmont. This time the journey home was to be as deck cargo on the Compagnie Generale Maritime container ship *La Perouse*. This Kerguelen Islands-registered vessel was built in 1988 and was 36,389grt. Travelling across the Pacific Ocean, the Panama Canal and the Atlantic Ocean, No 4472 completed her circumnavigation, arriving back in the UK on 14 December 1989.

**T**he first four months of 1990 were spent at Southall giving the locomotive a thorough check-over after her Australian exertions. The return to the main line was a special six-coach 'FSS Executive' on 2 May, from Didcot to Banbury, after which No 4472 was detached to run with just the support coach to Carnforth. This was to position the loco for a month of 'Sellafield Sightseer' trains, sponsored by BNFL. On 16 June No 4472 made her debut on the Crewe to Holyhead route with an 'Ynys Mon Express'. This train then ran three days each week between 1 July and 16 September. On 18 July No 4472 was hauling the train when tragedy struck – a passenger leaning out of an open window hit his head on a rocky outcrop while passing through Penmaenbach Tunnel and was killed instantly. The last main-line trip of the year was on 15 September, after which the locomotive was to be withdrawn for replacement of the small tubes. But first came an October first visit to the Severn Valley Railway.

The pattern previously established continued in 1991 with participation in the pool of locomotives working the 'North Wales Coast Express' (by now retitled the 'Ynys Mon Express') and the 'Welsh

Marches Express'. In between was a visit to Carlisle in April and attendance at the BR Coalville Open Day on 26 May. At the end of August a piston ring problem caused the locomotive to miss both a 'Welsh Marches' and 'Ynys Mon' trip, but this was repaired in time for a return visit to the Severn Valley Railway at the end of September. This was followed over 19/20 October by participation, with Nos 34027 and 70000, in the Network SouthEast-sponsored Fen Steam Weekend between Kings Lynn and Cambridge.

A new departure for 1992 was participation, with No 34027, in Carlisle to Keighley trips, hauling the 'Royal Scotsman' land cruise train. Also a special trip was run from Preston to Carlisle on 16 May as part of the Preston Guild celebrations. The high summer programme of 'Ynys Mon' and 'Cumbrian Mountain' trains continued as before, with a first visit to the National Railway Museum in late September and early October.

The seven-year main-line boiler 'ticket' expired on 27 November, so the locomotive moved back to Southall from Sheffield on 21 October, working a final 'Shakespeare' on the 25th. Although the main-line

During a visit to the Nene Valley Railway in July 1994 No 60103 provides a fine recreation of a typical East Coast fast freight from the 1960s. *D. Percival*

On 8 July 1994 No 60103 poses on the turntable at Wansford at the Nene Valley Railway, providing a good view of the locomotive in the late BR condition in which she appeared between 1993 and 1996. *D. Percival*

'ticket' is only valid for a maximum of seven years, the boiler insurance is valid for ten years, so the plan was to use the remaining three years of the boiler ticket operating and generating income on heritage railways.

A 1993 plan was devised that saw the locomotive move first to Tyseley in November 1992. Also during that month the spare second tender was sold to the new A1 Steam Locomotive Trust and moved from Southall to Morpeth. December saw the locomotive move by road to the Great Central Railway at Loughborough for participation in its 'Santa' services before a further movement in February to the East Lancashire Railway at Bury. March 1993 saw the No 4772 arrive at the Llangollen Railway. Unfortunately the steam test undertaken on arrival there revealed several leaking tubes and the locomotive had to be withdrawn from service. Future planned 1993 visits to the Severn Valley, Nene Valley, Paignton & Dartmouth and Gloucestershire Warwickshire railways all had to be cancelled.

An intermediate overhaul was undertaken at Southall through the summer of 1993, which saw the locomotive reappear in November in BR Brunswick green livery as No 60103 and visit Tyseley for a two-month stay. Visits to the Llangollen Railway (January to April 1994), Nene Valley Railway (May to July) and Swanage Railway (August) were followed by a visit to the Severn Valley Railway for the ceremonial reopening of the Kidderminster turntable on 23 September, before returning to Southall in October.

The following year began with a four-month return visit to the Llangollen Railway. Unfortunately this was marred by a complete derailment of the locomotive on sidings at Llangollen Goods Junction on 23 April 1995. An insurance inspection on the 25th found several cracks in the boiler and severe leaks in the foundation ring. The locomotive was again withdrawn from traffic and on 9 June returned to Southall by road. No 4472 had amassed a total of 30,000 miles running on private railways in the previous two years. With expiry of the 10-year boiler 'ticket' due in November 1995 and the locomotive requiring a two/three-year general overhaul estimated to cost £1.5 million, problems were beginning to mount up. Despite the mileage run on private railways, it is now clear that the operation of the locomotive during the five years since the return from Australia had severely depleted the funds available for its running and maintenance.

What was now Flying Scotsman Railways (FSR), as the parent company of Waterman Railways, had acquired the BR Special Trains Unit on 30 March 1995, with Bill McAlpine as Chairman and Pete Waterman as Chief Executive, and was clearly short of capital. Problems in the wider Flying Scotsman Railways Group were brought to a head in July and August when Roland Kennington was laid off at Southall and the Carriage & Wagon activity at Carnforth was closed down. With no paid staff at Southall and no budget for repairs, the situation looked bleak. Roland remained at Southall as a volunteer, with a small nucleus of supporters, thus ensuring that vandal attacks and damage were less likely. Media speculation regarding the future of the locomotive culminated in a front-page story in *Steam Railway* magazine, which was seen by Oxfordshire businessman Tony Marchington. Spurred on by the article, Dr Marchington rang Bill McAlpine and offered £1.25 million for the locomotive.

During the course of a visit to the Llangollen Railway in the spring of 1994, No 60103 emerges from Berwyn Tunnel with a train for Glydyfrdwy.
*D. Wilcock*

**D**r Tony Marchington was a longstanding steam enthusiast and the co-founder and CEO of the British biotechnology group Oxford Molecular Group plc, which was floated on the London Stock Exchange in 1994 for £30 million. By 1997 it was valued at £450 million. Apparently Dr Marchington had previously aspired to own an 'A4' 'Pacific' and had sought out the North American owners of both Nos 60010 *Dominion of Canada* and 60008 *Dwight D. Eisenhower*. The Canadian museum had apparently quoted a figure of around $3 million for No 60010. He had also spoken to the NELPG and Geoffrey Drury regarding the then unrestored No 60019 *Bittern*, and sums in excess of £325,000 had been mentioned. Dr Marchington had also approached the Severn Valley Railway regarding the possible sale of No 5690 *Leander*, and had been quoted £180,000 for this out-of-ticket Stanier 4-6-0. Apparently Bill McAlpine regarded the offer of £1.5 million for No 4472 as a very good price, and the availability of a further £1 million for the overhaul as the best way forward to secure the long-term future of the locomotive.

Accordingly plans were activated in February 1996 for Roland Kennington to formally resume leadership of the restoration team at Southall, to undertake a two-year overhaul and bring the locomotive back into service. The sale agreement was signed on 6 March 1996 and the £1.25 million price included the Southall depot and the set of Pullman cars that FSR had put up for sale in April 1995. Although it had been hoped that the locomotive could be ready for the 70th anniversary of the inaugural non-stop run of the 'Flying Scotsman' train in May 1998, the discovery of a cracked frame and the need for extensive boiler repairs so extended the work required as to make this unrealistic. One decision that was to have later repercussions was to replace the locomotive's vacuum brakes with air brakes only. Although at the time this was thought to be a future requirement for main-line operation, subsequently found to be only partially correct, this was to rule out any future operation on heritage lines, which continued to run only vacuum-braked stock.

In August 1996 the Flying Scotsman Association was launched through which supporters of the locomotive could, through an annual subscription of £20, help the restoration process, be allowed occasional access to the locomotive at Southall and be generally kept in touch with progress on the overhaul. Alan Pegler was appointed President of the Association. For the next three years these subscriptions, and a modest income from merchandising, was the only income accruing to FSR. Despite this, the directors were being paid significant sums in directors' fees. This was an ominous indication of things to come.

Eventually, at an estimated cost of almost £1 million, by June 1999 the overhaul was completed and the locomotive returned to traffic restored to apple green LNER livery and again running as No 4472, with the double chimney and Kylchap exhaust restored and also, for safety reasons, now carrying the German-style smoke deflectors that she had carried between 1961 and 1963. The test run was completed on 26 June on a Southall-Birmingham-Worcester-Oxford-Southall circuit, followed on 4 July by a triumphant first passenger trip from King's Cross to York, returning a week later.

A total of 16 main-line trips were operated in 1999. Four trips were run during the July to September period from London to Salisbury, followed by trips to Shrewsbury, Norwich and Yeovil. A special innovation was four trips in October, November and December recreating the old 'Shakespeare Express' formula, but this time starting at London Euston. Two trips were also run substituting for the non-available No 6024 *King Edward I*. Income in 1999 was therefore a respectable £430,000. Against this, administrative expenses were £352,000, and repairs and maintenance £95,000, with interest payments of £180,000, giving an annual loss of £520,000. With administrative expenses at 82% of income, this

Against the long shadows of a summer evening on Sunday 11 July 1999 No 4472 heads a return York to King's Cross excursion over Welwyn Viaduct. The outwards trip on the previous Sunday had been No 4472's first visit to King's Cross since 1969. *D. Percival*

established an unfortunate pattern that was to continue until the company failure in 2004, where the directors took fees out of all proportion to the locomotive's ability to earn income.

The year 2000 was to prove even more disastrous as a combination of factors saw only 11 trips run, with no fewer than 46 trips cancelled. Some of these trips were cancelled because of a period of high risk from lineside fires, but most were the consequence of Flying Scotsman Services' dismal failure to effectively market and price the trains, a contrast made even more sharp by Newmarket Travel sponsoring and running nine of the 11 trips that actually operated. The only bright spot was on 6 and 18 February, with the operation of the first two trips replacing the non-available No 35028 *Clan Line* hauling the prestigious Venice-Simplon Orient Express (VSOE) Pullman train. Income therefore slumped to only £198,000, with repairs and maintenance at £111,000, interest £260,000, and an annual loss of £560,000. Directors' fees were £46,000 (23% of turnover).

Also in 2000 Dr Marchington's business, Oxford Molecular, had declared losses of £26 million on a turnover of £20 million, and he had decided to liquidate its assets. Some £51 million was earned from asset sales to US companies, and shareholders obtained a return of 44p per share. With Dr Marchington's fortune somewhat depleted, his future ability to bankroll No 4472 was now in some doubt.

The following year, 2001, saw the full effects of the newly negotiated VSOE contract with a total of 41 trips undertaken, including no fewer than 22 with VSOE, and a further 10 hauling the associated 'Northern Belle' Pullman train. The new contract was to run from April 2001 for five years and included exclusive haulage of both the VSOE and 'Northern Belle' Pullman trains with flexibility to undertake additional work when not required for VSOE work. Total income for the year was £202,000, repairs and maintenance £90,000, interest £253,000 and administrative expenses £363,000, of which directors' fees were £149,000 (74% of turnover). The annual loss was £555,000. It is now clear that the VSOE contract may have been a prestigious one, but it generated insufficient income per trip when compared with more conventional work. Income per trip in 1999 was £26,000, but this had fallen to £18,000 in the 2000 season and a disastrous £4,900 in 2001. These figures are probably distorted by asset sales, as the Pullman cars were disposed of at this time for a total of £213,000. On-train sales of merchandise are a critical source of additional income to locomotive-owners, and it is now clear that the VSOE trains failed dismally in this respect, possibly because of competition from VSOE's own on-train sales.

Faced with large losses and the increased borrowings required to fund the continued operation of No 4472, the directors now came to a decision that was to prove financially advantageous for some of them, but disastrous for several thousand small investors – to float the company as a PLC. A prospectus was issued on 3 December 2001, which now (in 2010) makes interesting reading. It was based on three main strands. First was the hire agreement with VSOE and other earning potential. There was also reference to 'exhibition at preserved railways', recognising that the absence of vacuum brakes prevented the haulage of trains on these railways.

The details of the strategy also claimed 'that market research in 1999 and 2000 had indicated that a premium of up to £100 per passenger would be sustainable for steam rail excursions pulled by *Flying Scotsman* in the United Kingdom.' Given the very large number of cancellations experienced in 2000 as a result of uncompetitive pricing, this claim is difficult to sustain. It was also claimed that the number of VSOE trips were planned to increase in subsequent years. Given that 32 trips had been run in 2001, a significant increase would have been hard to sustain given other demands on the locomotive's availability and the need for some maintenance downtime.

Second was the new concept of a 'Flying Scotsman Village'. This was planned to be located in Edinburgh, adjacent to Waverley station, and that 'the locomotive will be physically present for a majority of the time at the proposed Flying Scotsman Village site'. The contradiction with the planned rise in the number of London- and York-based VSOE trips is not explained.

The third strand was the merchandising possibilities presented by the locomotive. In support of this the prospectus mentioned the Microsoft Train Simulator, which featured the locomotive. Elsewhere it was admitted that 'the Group derives no revenue from the agreement with Microsoft'! Also mentioned as possible income streams was the website and the 'Flying Scotsman Club 4472'.

It is difficult not to come to the conclusion that the Prospectus issued by the directors took a highly optimistic view of the commercial prospects for the locomotive, some of it apparent from a careful reading of the document, and the unfortunate investors were more likely to be motivated by sentiment than a real investment opportunity. And so it proved. The actual declared results for 2001 showed a shortfall of £17,000 on the estimated income of £219,000. The operating loss was estimated as £360,000, and the actual declared loss was £555,000. The directors took fees of £149,000 (74% of turnover). The audit report contained an ominous statement, specifically drawing attention to 'uncertainty as to the ability of the Group to generate income from unproven new products and sources'.

The next year, 2002, proved to be no better. Although the VSOE operation generated 25 trips,

with a further six 'Northern Belle' trips, five VSOE trips ran with diesels and on 10 July No 4472 actually failed at Theale while hauling a Bristol trip. A further two 'Northern Belle' trips ran with diesels and no fewer than nine were cancelled. VSOE had adopted a practice of charging a premium for steam haulage and clearly this was meeting customer resistance, particularly with the 'Northern Belle' train. A further four non-VSOE trips were planned, of which only two actually ran. Financially the year proved no less disastrous the previous year, turnover being only slightly up at £238,000 and the declared loss slightly down at £474,000. Again the directors took £161,000, 68% of turnover.

The year 2003 began with the onset of mechanical problems that were to dog No 4772 for most of the early part of the year. Because of her non-availability, the 'Northern Belle' part of the VSOE contract was lost to No 6233 *Duchess of Sutherland*, which commenced working these trains from 29 March. Many VSOE trips out of London were worked by either No 60009 *Union of South Africa* (five trips), No 34027 *Taw Valley* (four trips), or diesels (14 trips).

Although some 16 VSOE trips were actually worked by No 4472, the locomotive's failure to appear on so many others caused a severe loss of confidence, not helped by a failure at Doncaster on 30 July when working from York to King's Cross for Pathfinder Tours. Fire risk was an issue in August and September, together with an English, Welsh & Scottish Railway (EWS) industrial dispute on 4 October, but the efforts of Roland and his team at Southall had to wait until October before the locomotive regained her former reliability, running seven trips in December.

This caused turnover for 2003 to decline to only £51,000, leaving an annual loss of £390,000, yet the directors still took £107,000, 210% of turnover.

Although 2004 began satisfactorily, with three VSOE trips run in January, the mechanical problems returned with a trip on 3 March being diesel-hauled because of a hot box on No 4472. In fact, the 10 January trip was the very last VSOE outing to be hauled by No 4472 herself, with three further VSOE trips hauled by No 34067 *Tangmere* before she herself failed on 22 March.

By now the decision to sell the locomotive had become public, and Roland Kennington and his team had to work at Southall under a storm of media interest. The dedication of Roland, who was never a director of Flying Scotsman Railways and therefore never shared in the largess that the directors allocated to themselves, should not go unrecorded. On a number of occasions towards the end, that the locomotive appeared at all was down to his preparedness to pay for the necessary coal and water out of his own resources, Flying Scotsman Railways having run out of credit.

Although there was some interest within the UK, fears were expressed in the media that she could be sold abroad. Accordingly a public appeal was launched, coordinated by the NRM, to seek contributions in order to buy the locomotive 'for the nation'. This was bolstered by an offer from Richard Branson to match pound-for-pound the public contributions, backed by £1.8 million from the National Heritage Memorial Fund and topped up with £600,000 from regional development agency Yorkshire Forward. The appeal eventually raised £365,000 in public donations, matched by a similar sum from Richard Branson.

During the period when No 4472 was engaged by Orient Express for haulage of the UK Pullman train, on 10 November 2001 No 4472 crosses Digswell Viaduct with the Victoria to Royston 'VSOE Pullman'. *D. Percival*

The final price was £2.3 million, paid in April 2004. Despite Roland's best efforts, No 4472 continued with her mechanical problems and burst a tube before the planned movement from Doncaster to York on 29 May, and was unavailable for three trips in July and August. For her triumphant entry into the 'Railfest' at the NRM in May 2004 she had to be pushed by a diesel. However, before the end of the year she did manage 14 days of NRM-sponsored trips between York and Scarborough.

The FSR annual report for 2003, published on 23 December 2004, revealed the final cancellation of the 'Flying Scotsman Village' project and admitted that the reduced income from the VSOE contract was generating insufficient cash to support the business and was, in particular, insufficient to ensure payment of the outstanding bank loans. The Board had decided therefore to sell the locomotive and wind down the business. During the previous five years the directors had given themselves £497,000 in fees, while the business had racked up total losses of £2.5 million.

This was to be the last year of No 4472's operation as the boiler

'ticket' expired in December. The NRM sponsored a series of 32 York to Scarborough trips marketed as 'Ride the Legend Express' in June, July, August and September 2004. However, No 4472's increasingly fragile condition caused a total of seven days of workings to hauled by other locomotives. In October 2004 the locomotive moved to Tyseley for a series of 'final journey' trips marketed by Vintage Trains, with two trips to Didcot in October, then a final series of completely sold-out Christmas Lunch trips during 15, 16 and 17 December over a circular Birmingham-Leicester-Burton-Birmingham route. The final trip was to be on 18 December, but again No 4472 proved reluctant to rise to the occasion and was failed, so this train was worked to Didcot and back by No 4965 *Rood Ashton Hall*.

*Flying Scotsman* then returned to York and the process of stripping down began. One key decision was made early on in the overhaul. First, the firebox was removed from the boiler as it was suspected that severe deterioration had set in. This proved to be accurate and work stopped for three months while options were evaluated. The NRM had acquired with the locomotive the spare boiler, No 27020, which had been removed in 1978. The boiler removed from the locomotive was ex-'A4' boiler No 27971. Because of the latter's poor condition it was decided to recover 'A3' boiler No 27020 from Southall and refurbish that for future use on No 4472. However, it had not been carefully stored during the 24 years since it was last used, and this was to prove a source of much delay and extra expense as the overhaul progressed. A second key decision was to reinstate vacuum brakes, so that the locomotive can haul trains once again on heritage railways. The NRM has received much criticism from armchair critics who do not seem to realise that one only has a very imprecise knowledge of future work requirements when beginning to overhaul a locomotive boiler. It is also the general experience that a boiler overhaul usually ends up costing more and taking longer than when it commenced.

Anxious not to waste an opportunity to generate some additional funds, in 2008 the NRM approached all British 'A4' locomotive owners to see if there was any interest in purchasing boiler 27971, and in 2009 its sale was announced to the owner of No 60019 *Bittern*, Jeremy Hosking, for £27,000. The £850,000 overhaul of boiler 27020, originally estimated at only £400,000, was contracted to Roger Pridham at his works in Tavistock, Devon, in a contract shared with Ian Riley at Bury, with the mechanical work being undertaken by the NRM's own staff at York. The new inner copper firebox throatplate experienced some problems with welds failing final inspection, before final movement for retubing to Ian Riley's works at Bury in February 2009. The latest estimated cost of the overhaul is now £1.3 million, with completion expected in mid-2011. This has caused some problems with the Heritage Lottery Fund, as its funding contribution carries a deadline, already extended once, of June 2010 for the completion of the project. It is to be hoped that, once completed, the locomotive will resume her place as the holder of several world records, and as the most famous steam locomotive in Britain and possibly the English-speaking world.

*Overleaf:* One of the most spectacular sights during the Australian visit was on 6 August 1989 when the opportunity was taken to run No 4472 north from Melbourne to Seymour on the triple-track standard/broad gauge section in parallel with two broad gauge 4-6-4 locomotives Nos 761 and 707. Apparently the sound was deafening, as can well be imagined by this spectacular view, as under threatening skies the three trains climb the 1 in 50 gradient towards Heathcote Junction, Victoria. *Robert Carlisle*

*Understanding*
# PARKINSON'S
## DISEASE

**Dr JMS Pearce**

Published by Family Doctor Publications Limited
in association with the British Medical Association

**IMPORTANT**

This book is intended to supplement the advice given to you by your doctor. The author and publisher have taken every care in its preparation. In particular, information about drugs and dosages has been thoroughly checked. However, before taking any medication you are strongly advised to read the product information sheet accompanying it. Your pharmacist will be able to help you with anything you do not understand.

© Family Doctor Publications 1995

**Medical Editor:** Dr Tony Smith
**Consultant Editor:** Anne Patterson
**Medical Artist:** Angela Christie
**Design:** Fox Design, Bramley, Guildford, Surrey
**Printing**: Cambus Litho, Scotland, using acid-free paper

**ISBN: 1 898205 12 4**

# Contents

# AN

# ESSAY

## ON THE

# SHAKING PALSY.

---

BY

### *JAMES PARKINSON,*

MEMBER OF THE ROYAL COLLEGE OF SURGEONS.

---

### *LONDON:*

PRINTED BY WHITTINGHAM AND ROWLAND,
*Goswell Street,*

FOR SHERWOOD, NEELY, AND JONES,

PATERNOSTER ROW.

1817.

James Parkinson (1775-1824), who first described the disease, practised as a GP in Hoxton, a suburb of Shoreditch, London. A great social reformer, author, celebrated biologist and geologist, his ' Essay on the Shaking Palsy', containing descriptions of six of his patients, was published in 1817.

# Introduction

If you, or a close relative or friend, suffer from Parkinson's disease, this book is written for you. It is aimed to help you to understand the symptoms and disabilities caused by the disease and to suggest what you can do for yourself as well as what doctors can do to treat the condition. The good news is that, although there is still much to be learned, the grim prospects which prevailed 30 years ago have been improved by increased understanding and modern treatments.

## WHAT IS PARKINSON'S DISEASE?

Parkinson's disease is characterised by a collection of signs involving the nervous system, the most important of which are:

- slowness of movement
- rigidity — the limbs may feel heavy and stiff

- shaking (tremor) of the hands and sometimes legs at rest
- disorders of posture — the patient's neck and trunk assume a bent position, and the arms fail to swing freely when walking.

The disease is caused by degeneration of pigmented nerve cells in the brain. It usually starts in the fifties or sixties and can remain stationary for months or years, but usually progresses. Parkinson's disease seldom shortens life expentancy to any significant degree.

In the advanced stages, tremor, slowness and rigidity may affect all four limbs and the trunk; speech may be indistinct and slurred, the limbs and body are bent, and the victim is prone to walk with short, stumbling steps and is prone to fall.

## WHO GETS IT?

The illness may afflict people from all classes of society, from all races, and occurs throughout the world. It increases with ageing, but is not caused by ageing itself. Overall, about one person in 1000 is affected, but this increases to about one in 100 people in their seventies and eighties. Many elderly people are so mildly affected that the condition is easily overlooked. Men and women are equally affected, and the disease is seldom inherited.

### Don't get too depressed

If this description sounds depressing, remember that for many years, the disability is mild and during this time most patients are capable of normal domestic activities and can usually maintain their normal jobs. Furthermore, although there is no cure for Parkinson's disease, many of the symptoms can be controlled by appropriate treatment.

## HOW IS THE DIAGNOSIS MADE?

People wonder how the diagnosis is made. It is invariably a clinical decision, based on the symptoms and especially the signs that the experienced doctor can observe during examination. Laboratory tests and X-rays are generally unnecessary, and special tests such as computerised tomography (CT) scans and magnetic resonance imaging (MRI) scans are generally unhelpful; indeed they are often normal in Parkinson's disease.

## HOW IS PARKINSON'S DISEASE TREATED?

Treatment is based on the replacement of those chemicals in the brain that are reduced or depleted by Parkinson's disease. The main chemical affected by Parkinson's disease is dopamine, which diminishes slowly for many years before any symptoms are apparent. It is estimated that you have to lose 80 per cent of the dopamine in the critical areas of your brain before symptoms or signs are evident. Dopamine is found in groups of nerve cells in the base of the brain, called the basal ganglia. Patients are given a drug called levodopa to replace the missing dopamine, but other drugs are used too.

### Physical therapies

Physical treatment with physiotherapy, speech and occupational therapy are valuable at certain stages. They supplement, but are not an effective substitute for, drug treatment. The aim throughout is to maintain your activity and as near-normal a lifestyle as possible.

### Who will treat you?

Patients and their families have to be as active as the doctors and therapists. Your GP will be the first person to consult and indeed may assume responsibility for managing your condition, including making the diagnosis, explaining and prescribing drugs, and possibly organising physiotherapy and occupational therapy. The GP may then refer you to a consultant, ideally a neurologist, although it could be a general physician or a geriatrician. The consultant will write to your GP confirming the diagnosis and advising him or her about treatment.

Once the diagnosis has been confirmed and treatment started, the GP will provide continuing care, although he or she will probably refer you back to the consultant if any problems arise.

## KEY POINTS

✓ Parkinson's disease can affect people from all races and social classes, and men and women are equally affected.

✓ The illness is more common in elderly people.

✓ Symptoms can be controlled by appropriate treatment.

# Causes & characteristics

The essential cause is not known. Clues are available from studies of the distribution of the disease, that is, who is affected, where, and in what circumstances. I have already mentioned that it is relatively common—perhaps as many as 100,000 patients are affected in the UK at any one time—that men and women are equally affected, and that no race is immune. It is not related to any particular job and is clearly a physical disease of the brain, which is not caused by stress, anxiety, emotional or family upsets. Extensive searches for a viral or bacterial cause have proved negative, so the disease is not infectious.

## NERVE CELLS IN THE BRAIN ARE AFFECTED

In patients with Parkinson's disease, there is disease or degeneration of the so-called basal ganglia in the deeper grey matter of the brain, particularly of that part known as the substantia nigra.

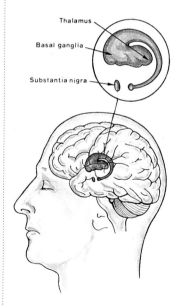

Thalamus

Basal ganglia

Substantia nigra

In Parkinson's disease, there is degeneration of the substantia nigra which produces the chemical dopamine deep inside the brain.

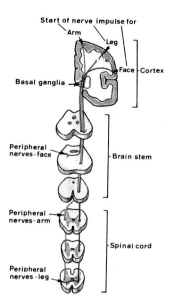

Various parts of the nervous system combine to generate movement. Nerve impulses start in the cortex, pass through the basal ganglia, brain stem and spinal cord and finally pass through the peripheral nerves which actually control muscles.

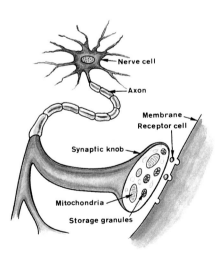

Dopamine is released from storage granules in the nerve cell, travels down the axon across the synaptic knob to dopamine receptors at the *next* nerve cell.

The substantia nigra, which connects with the striatum (caudate nucleus and globus pallidus) contains black pigmented cells and, in normal individuals, produces a number of chemical transmitters, the most important of which is dopamine. Other transmitters include serotonin, somatostatin and noradrenaline. In Parkinson's disease, the basal ganglia cells produce less dopamine, which is needed to transmit vital messages to other parts of the brain, and to the spinal cord, nerves and muscles.

The basal ganglia, through the action of dopamine, are responsible for planning and controlling automatic movements of the body, such as pointing with a finger, pulling on a sock, writing or walking. If the basal ganglia are not working properly, as in Parkinson's disease patients, all aspects of movement are impaired, resulting in the characteristic features of the disease—slowness of movement, stiffness and effort required to move a limb and, often, tremor.

Dopamine levels in the brain's substantia nigra do normally fall with ageing. However, they have to fall to one-fifth of normal values for the symptoms and signs of Parkinsonism to emerge.

### An important balance

Normally, there is a balance between dopamine and another neurotransmitter called acetylcholine. Acetylcholine is present in many areas of the brain and plays a part in normal memory recording and recall. Because dopamine is depleted, there is a relative excess of acetylcholine. Thus two of the main groups of drugs used to treat Parkinson's disease are dopamine drugs (levodopa and its preparations Madopar and Sinemet) and drugs designed to restore the balance by diminishing the acetylcholine—anticholinergics (for example, Artane, Disipal, Cogentin).

### How do the nerve cells send messages?

The diagram opposite shows how the nerve cells or neurones in the basal ganglia release packages of the dopamine, transmit it down its main wire or axon and how this sprouts into receptors of the next nerve cells and transmits the message and nerve impulse further down the line. You can imagine this process carried out by millions of neurones at the same time, forming a network of activity which puts BT to shame.

### Receptors are important

The receptors are most important. Some drugs can block the receptors, and if they are taken for a long period they block the passage of dopamine in the nerve cells and their connecting network of axons. The nerve impulses so essential for normal movements are therefore reduced. This is the basis of the drug-induced Parkinsonism I shall describe next.

## AGEING AND HEREDITY

Although Parkinson's disease is not caused by the normal ageing process that affects all our brains, just as it does other organs, the incidence of the disease does increase as we get older. A family history is obtained in five to 10 per cent of patients, but studies on twins suggest that hereditary factors are relatively unimportant. It may be that affected relatives share some environmental agent or are genetically vulnerable to it. What this environmental factor might be, we do not know.

## KEY POINTS

✓ The cause of Parkinson's disease is unknown.

✓ Research has shown that pigment-containing cells in the deep part of the brain that produce dopamine and other important chemicals degenerate and die. This, in turn, affects the working of other parts of the brain, the spinal cord, nerves and muscles involved in movement.

✓ When the chemical dopamine is depleted, there is a relative excess of the chemical acetylcholine.

✓ Treatment is aimed at boosting dopamine levels and/or diminishing acetylcholine levels.

# Types of Parkinsonism

We separate Parkinson's disease (idiopathic Parkinson's disease or paralysis agitans) described by James Parkinson in 1817 from a group of rarer disorders also caused by impairment of the function of the nerve cells of the brain and called secondary or symptomatic Parkinsonism.

There are several kinds of symptomatic Parkinsonism:

- drug-induced Parkinsonism
- so-called post-encephalitic Parkinsonism
- progressive supranuclear palsy
- poison-induced Parkinsonism

It is important to distinguish between true Parkinson's disease and symptomatic Parkinsonism because the treatment may be different.

## DRUG-INDUCED PARKINSONISM

Neuroleptic drugs used in the treatment of schizophrenia and other serious psychotic mental illnesses can block the release or transmission of dopamine in the substantia nigra and striatum, causing Parkinsonism. The most common neuroleptic drugs are the phenothiazines, but there are many others, as shown in the table on the next page. The list is not complete, and if in doubt, you should ask your GP or consultant whether the drug you are taking might cause Parkinsonism.

Some of these drugs are used to counter nausea, vomiting or dizziness and in these circumstances Parkinsonism should not develop if the course of treatment is restricted to less than a month for these symptoms. If it is possible for your physician to withdraw the drugs, the Parkinsonism will usually slowly disappear, though this may take several months. Some patients with serious psychiatric illness need to continue the neuroleptic drugs; some degree of Parkinsonism then has to be tolerated to maintain mental stability, and can usually be controlled.

## POST-ENCEPHALITIC PARKINSONISM

This type of Parkinsonism is now extremely rare. It developed in the wake of a diffuse inflammation of the brain (encephalitis) caused by an epidemic of a particular virus infection which raged throughout the world between 1918 and 1926. The symptoms and treatment are slightly different from those of idiopathic Parkinson's disease.

## PROGRESSIVE SUPRA-NUCLEAR PALSY AND OTHER TYPES OF PARKINSONISM

Parkinsonism is not normally a feature of head injury and is seldom a symptom of a brain tumour. Similar rigid-akinetic states can result from a variety of other degenerations of the brain, including the conditions known as progressive supranuclear palsy, multi-system atrophies, and Lewy body disease. All these conditions are rare causes of Parkinsonism and require specialised neurological assessment; they do not all respond well to anti-Parkinsonian drugs.

## POISONS-INDUCED PARKINSONISM

It has been found that MPTP, a chemical contaminant of do-it-yourself drugs made illegally and used by heroin addicts, mainly in California, can produce Parkinsonism within days or weeks. The brains in fatal cases show severe destruction of the substantia nigra and profound loss of dopamine and other neural transmitters as is seen in Parkinson's disease.

Their symptoms are controlled by levodopa drugs, which replace the missing dopamine in just the same way as in Parkinson's disease. However, the brain damage inflicted by MPTP is permanent. Researchers now have proof that certain poisons can damage the brain in a way similar to that arising spontaneously in idiopathic Parkinson's disease—a valuable finding for further research into the sequence of events leading to degeneration of the dopamine-generating cells. For example, in animal experiments in which Parkinsonism is artificially induced using MPTP, it has been shown that the dopamine-producing cells in the substantia nigra are deficient in one of the important enzymes known as complex-1, involved in oxygen control in the cell.

In spite of improved knowledge and understanding of the nature and causes of Parkinson's disease, more work needs to be done to further our knowledge and to develop better treatment.

## KEY POINTS

✓ Parkinson's disease needs to be distinguished from various types of symptomatic Parkinsonism because the treatment may be different.

# Symptoms and signs

I have mentioned earlier, the principal symptoms of Parkinson's disease are tremor, muscular rigidity, akinesia, abnormal posture and loss of balance. Let's look at these in more detail.

Shaking of one or both hands is the commonest early symptom.

- Tremor. The commonest early symptom is shaking (tremor) of one or both hands. It occurs at rest and is reduced or stopped when the limb is in action. It is fairly slow—about five beats per second and is rhythmical. It usually vanishes during sleep.
- Rigidity. By rigidity is meant stiffness and a sense of effort required to move the limb, which may feel heavy and weak. However, loss of strength and power is not a feature of Parkinson's disease.
- Akinesia. Slowness of movement is experienced in three ways: lack of spontaneous movement (akinesia), slowness in starting a movement, and slowness during the movement (bradykinesia). The handwriting becomes progressively smaller (micrographia: micro - small, graphos - writing) and may show the tremor.

Dear Dr. Pearce,

This is to authorise you to prepare a report on my medical condition in relation to my ability to drive safely, and to send it to the DVLA.

Yours truly,

Characteristically small handwriting of a patient with Parkinson's disease.

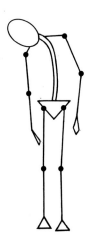

- Disorders of posture. Disorders of posture refer to the bent position of the neck and trunk that develops late in the disease and describes the way the arms are held close to the sides, elbows and wrists slightly bent; the legs, too, may be flexed at the hips and knees.

Characteristic posture disorders.

A walk may break into a run. This is called 'festination'.

- Loss of balance. This commonly accompanies disordered posture. Patients find it difficult to correct a trip or stumble (lack of righting reflexes) and as a consequence are prone to fall. They seem to lean forward in front of their centre of gravity and, without being able to help themselves, a walk may break into a run (called festination by doctors, from the Latin festinare: to hurry). Or, if pushed gently, patients may uncontrollably run forwards or stumble backwards.

Symptoms vary a great deal. For example, some patients never develop a tremor.

## SIGNS

When your doctor examines you he will notice certain signs, though as with the symptoms, these vary much from patient to patient, and change in the individual at different times. Your movements may be visibly slow (bradykinesia: brady - slow, kinesis - movement). You may rise slowly from the chair or walk slowly with short steps into the consulting room. You may have a slow rhythmic tremor of one or both arms which disappears on grasping a chair or taking hold of an object. Many years ago this was likened to rolling pills made by hand: pill rolling tremor. When the doctor bends or straightens your wrist or arm or legs he may feel a sense of resistance like trying to bend a lead pipe; he may also feel the tremor superimposed, creating a sensation of turning a cogwheel (known as cogwheel rigidity).

### SOME COMMON SYMPTOMS AND SIGNS OF PARKINSON'S DISEASE

- Difficulty fastening buttons
- Can't turn over
- Can't get up from chair
- Expressionless face
- Falls frequently
- Feet freeze
- Greasy skin
- Rarely blinks
- Shuffling steps
- Slow eating
- Slow movement
- Soft voice
- Stiff limbs
- Tremor

### Automatic movements are reduced

Actions are noticeably laboured. Most of us perform automatic movements unconsciously at rest, when sitting comfortably. Such movements, blinking, crossing and uncrossing the legs, and general fidgeting, for example, are lacking in the Parkinson's patient. When walking, Parkinson's disease patients use short steps and shuffle, as if the feet are glued to the floor. Gait is hesitant and steps shorten even more in doorways or when there is an obstruction, or if in the street, a passing dog or a stranger runs across their path. Sometimes patients get stuck when walking; their feet feel frozen to the ground. If this happens to you, deliberately focus on a spot in front and aim at it with the leading leg: you will find you can usually start to walk again.

## Facial appearance and speech are altered

The face may lack expression, the eyes are a little staring, and in advanced cases there is a tendency to dribble saliva. This arises, not because of excessive formation, but because of reduction in the normal swallowing of saliva that we do unconsciously and automatically. The voice is quiet, sometimes hoarse (dysphonia) and the words may be slurred (dysarthria). These problems may be inconspicuous, but may present with difficulty singing in the bath or, more embarrassingly, in the choir.

## Bladder and bowel habits change

Constipation is almost invariable. It is caused by sluggish movement of the muscle in the bowel, very similar to that seen in the limbs. It is not a serious symptom, but it does cause much concern and apprehension, particularly in the elderly. The bladder muscle, too, contracts less efficiently, and frequent calls to pass urine are common, with small volumes and some measure of urgency. In older men, coincidental enlargement of the prostate may add to the problems, with a slow stream and the need to get up at night to pass urine.

If you have these problems, you may need to be assessed by both a neurologist and a urologist. Incontinence does not occur in the early stages of the illness and if it does occur later, it may have some other explanation. You may have accidents because of physical slowness, being unable to get to the toilet in time; this is not true incontinence but urgency incontinence that can sometimes be improved by drugs such as oxybutinin.

## Swallowing may be difficult

Occasionally, difficulty in swallowing develops as a result of the illness, but special tests are needed to make sure this symptom is not due to causes other than Parkinsonism, which have arisen by chance.

## Some other problems

Usually, these are late features which appear after many years of illness. Most patients are able to walk well, to speak clearly and to work and enjoy leisure activities for many years. Modern specialist treatment by a neurologist controls symptoms effectively in most sufferers.

Other problems occasionally trouble patients. Pain is not a serious problem for most sufferers, though aching and stiffness in the neck, back and limbs is quite common. Because of reduced automatic movement, a stiff or frozen shoulder may develop. This is painful and stops men getting to their wallets in their back trouser pockets and causes women difficulties with zips and bra fasteners. These incidental problems can be treated effectively. Rarely, patients are affected by writer's cramp. Treatment with drugs can also cause symptoms.

## KEY POINTS

✓ Symptoms of Parkinson's disease include tremor, rigidity, akinesia, disorders of posture and loss of balance.

✓ Symptoms vary a great deal and later in the illness may include changed bladder and bowel habits and difficulty in swallowing.

✓ Signs include reduced automatic movements, altered facial appearance and speech.

# How is the diagnosis made?

Some patients, and even more of their relations, worry about the accuracy of the diagnosis. One patient differs from the next and your symptoms and your appearance may be different from those of the chap shaking away in your local or in the corner shop, who is said to have Parkinson's disease. In most cases an accurate diagnosis is not difficult.

As with certain other diseases, there are no specific or diagnostic tests that confirm or refute the diagnosis. Blood tests, electroencephalograms (EEG), computed tomography (CT) and magnetic resonance imaging (MRI) scans are essentially normal.

Parkinson's disease can be mistaken for other diseases, and because the outlook and treatment may be substantially different, it is generally advisable for the initial suspicion to be confirmed or rejected by a consultant neurologist. The diagnosis is based on the history and signs, and to the expert eye, may be immediately evident when the patient enters the consulting room. A change in handwriting, dragging of one leg without hip disease, or a complaint of clumsiness will all alert the doctor to the possible diagnosis. The severity and the type of illness will be explored in this clinical examination and the disability will be shown by questioning about what you can and cannot do.

## WHAT OTHER CONDITIONS LOOK LIKE PARKINSON'S DISEASE?

You can see from the table on page 20 that other causes of shaking and tremors can be mistaken for Parkinson's disease. The most frequent is a common, fairly harmless condition called benign essential tremor, which occurs in two to four per cent of the population, in varying degree. Here, the shaking is slight or absent at rest but worse when the arms are held stretched out; there is usually no rigidity or slowness of movement and no tendency to a bent or flexed posture. It often, but not always, runs in families, and the tremor may be reduced by a small dose of alcohol. It does not respond to anti-Parkinsonian drugs.

Thyroid disease, alcoholism, anxiety states and a variety of rare metabolic and structural disorders can occasionally mimic Parkinson's disease but these will be suspected by the specialist if the symptoms are unusual, and it is only then that investigations may be suggested. These conditions are rarely a diagnostic problem, so tests are not undertaken in most patients.

**Multiple sclerosis and strokes**
Occasionally, people who are subsequently diagnosed as having Parkinson's disease wonder if it is multiple sclerosis or some form of unusual stroke. Multiple sclerosis is mainly a disease of younger people, and its symptoms and signs are quite different and will be quickly appreciated by the specialist.

Multiple strokes affecting in turn each side of the body can rarely produce a picture that superficially resembles Parkinson's disease; here, expert opinion will separate the two conditions. There is, of course, nothing to prevent

both conditions arising by chance in the same unfortunate individual, but the specialist will usually be able to clarify the issue. Strokes do not, however, cause Parkinson's disease.

## CONDITIONS THAT LOOK LIKE PARKINSON'S DISEASE

- Post-encephalitic Parkinsonism; drug-induced Parkinsonism
- Other causes of tremor—benign familial tremor; thyrotoxicosis, alcoholism
- Other brain disease—multiple strokes

**Diseases not to be confused with Parkinson's disease**
- Brain tumour
- Strokes
- Multiple sclerosis
- After-effects of head injury
- Alzheimer's disease and primary dementias
- Motor neurone disease

**Is it Alzheimer's disease?**
Sometimes the more advanced or elderly patient may suffer from loss of memory or develop periods of confusion. The family rightly ask, "Is he becoming demented?" "Is

he developing Alzheimer's disease?"Patients with Alzheimer's disease and the superficially similar Lewy body disease have mental symptoms of forgetfulness and poor judgement from the beginning, whereas in Parkinson's disease the early symptoms are physical slowness, stiffness or tremor. Although the symptoms of Alzheimer's and Parkinson's overlap and resemble each other, neurologists can usually distinguish these conditions on clinical grounds, sometimes supplemented by brain scans and other tests.

## KEY POINTS

✓ In most cases an accurate diagnosis is not difficult.

✓ Parkinson's disease should not be confused with, and is not caused by, multiple sclerosis or strokes.

✓ People with Alzheimer's disease have mental symptoms from the beginning whereas the early symptoms in Parkinson's disease are physical slowness, stiffness or tremor.

# Does Parkinson's disease affect the mind?

Nervous and emotional factors play their part in all human disease. The effects of worry and sleeplessness in worsening the pain of even a minor bruise or toothache are as well knows as the harmful effects of personal worries on the symptoms of, for example, asthma or a stomach ulcer. Conversely, if you have a physical illness such as a broken leg, bronchitis, a breast lump or Parkinson's disease, it is not surprising if you feel anxious, apprehensive or even depressed about it.

The most obvious psychological accompaniments of Parkinson's disease are anxiety or depression caused by the physical symptoms of the disease and the disability it produces. Tremor and ponderous slow movements are a source of social embarrassment. An abnormal gait, trips and falls, difficulty with speech and voice also embarrass the sufferer. At a very late stage, after many years, the physical handicaps can be severe and restrict many activities; it is no wonder that patients then feel despondent and depressed, particularly about their dependence on others. Fears of future incapacity add to their worries.

## DEPRESSION

A depressive illness occurs at some time in about one-third of all Parkinson's disease patients. Depressive illness here means symptoms out of proportion to the underlying cause, or symptoms of such severity that the patient can't cope with them. Depression can occur out of the blue when there is no apparent stress, source of anxiety or physical disability to explain it. This is call endogenous depression. It is of interest that the incidence is higher than in people without Parkinson's disease even before the physical signs of Parkinson's disease are apparent.

## Symptoms of depression

If you have ever been depressed you will remember the feelings of being miserable, unhappy and low in spirits; you probably also remember the apathy, being devoid of vitality, interests and enthusiasms. Being depressed is quite different from the common complaint of being bored, anxious or just fed up, so commonly expressed by those who are young, disillusioned and unemployed. Depressed patients have to push themselves to make the effort to do everyday tasks; getting dressed, shaving or putting on make up, going out, mixing socially or even having a chat with family or friends. Life seems pointless, hopeless and futile. Sleep is disturbed. Patients go to bed early, to get away from it all, sleep fitfully till 4 or 5 a.m. and then can sleep no more. Early mornings are the worst time and by evenings the blues may have receded, a little. These diurnal swings of mood are characteristic.

Physical symptoms of vague pains, headaches, backache, palpitations and often a fear of cancer may dominate their lives, adding to the mental miseries. Feelings of wholly inappropriate guilt are mixed with a sense of inadequacy; if you are depressed, you blame yourself for all your family's misfortunes and sometimes for the evils of the world. You will feel periods of restlessness and agitation.

If you feel like this, you need medical attention. Depressed people may commit suicide but this is fortunately rare in Parkinson's disease.

## Treating depression is worthwhile

Symptoms generally respond well to antidepressant drugs of the tricyclic group (amitriptyline, dothiepin, etc.) but they must be supervised by your GP or specialist. They do not interact with anti-Parkinsonian drugs. Newer antidepressive drugs are of equal value and include the much-publicised paroxitene (Prozac). Treatment is usually necessary for six to 12 months, sometimes longer. Results are generally good.

## CONFUSION AND HALLUCINATIONS

These symptoms are uncommon both in younger patients and in the early stages of the disease. Don't forget that many people over the age of 70 have periods of memory lapses, disorientation and confusion. Deafness and impaired vision can lead to hallucinations in people without Parkinson's disease. When they occur in Parkinson's disease they may be the result of ageing effects alone, or they may be caused by drugs. Anti-Parkinsonian drugs of all types may cause disorientation, confusion and hallucinations. The most common ones are anticholinergic drugs, for example benzhexol (Artane), orphenadrine (Disipal), benztropine (Cogentin), but bromocriptine (Parlodel) and levodopa drugs (Madopar, Sinemet) can also cause confusional states.

## What happens?

Nightmares and frequent dreams are early warnings of these unpleasant side-effects. In most instances these problems come and go intermittently, but always tend to be more noticeable at night, in strange surroundings, such as hospitals or nursing homes. Disorientation may be related to time, place or person. The patient is bewildered and does not know where she is, nor what time of day it is. Recent information is imperfectly registered, so that the patient may deny having had lunch an hour ago, or forget having seen a recent visitor.

Visual hallucinations consist of seeing things that are not there: seeing people, faces, insects or animals. Auditory hallucinations consist of hearing sounds or voices that are not there: a radio or TV may seem to emit voices or they may seem to come from inside the patient's head. Sometimes the victim knows they are unreal, having insight into these intrusions sometimes he

or she may believe them to be real. They can cause distress and agitation.

Confusion may betray itself in peculiar conversation or strange erratic behaviour. Patients may wander off and get lost. They are often inattentive, distractable and memory appears poor because they seem unable to concentrate. Alternatively, they might pour milk into the teapot, put on clothes back to front, attempt to eat puddings with a knife or find themselves unable to tie a knot in their tie, or to use a comb or razor. These latter difficulties are technically called apraxia: the inability to perform skilled movements and sequences when the limbs have normal powers of strength, coordination and sensation.

## Drug effects

Although these symptoms may occur in demented patients and are often not totally curable, they may just be a sign of sensitivity to drugs. The doctor will reduce or gradually tail off any possible offending drug and symptoms will generally disappear. Obviously, reduction of anti-Parkinsonian treatment may lead to an increase in the slowness and rigidity of the disease, but in the end it is easier to handle a sane but physically slow patient than a more mobile confused one. A fine balance of drugs, tailored to the individual's needs will often provide a satisfactory if not perfect solution.

## DEMENTIA

One of the big worries about Parkinson's disease is that it is known to be associated with dementia—a decline in intellect, memory and the ability to make rational decisions and judgements. This has, without doubt, been overemphasised. Many Parkinsonian patients are not affected in this way and never become demented.

In later life both Parkinson's disease and Alzheimer's disease, the most frequent cause of dementia, are common. At the age of 70, about five to 10 per cent of the population show some signs of dementia, and about half of these will suffer from Alzheimer's disease. Thus there is a chance that some patients, purely by coincidence, have both Parkinsonism and dementia.

The combination is obviously unfortunate and the outlook is considerably worse. Coincidence apart, it is known that about 10 to 20 per cent of Parkinson's disease patients will develop dementia. If the dementing illness is apparent at the outset, the outlook is worse. If such patients are given levodopa drugs for their Parkinsonian symptoms; they can tolerate only small doses, and are prone to side-effects, particularly confusional states and hallucinations. In other words, dementia limits the amount of levodopa it is possible to give, and the control of Parkinsonian symptoms is less satisfactory for this reason.

The combination of Parkinson's disease and dementia is ultimately disabling. Families will need all the welfare services possible to cope with the patient at home. Ultimately, periods in longer-term hospitals or private nursing homes may be necessary. Research in this very difficult area is active and there is every hope that progress will be made.

## KEY POINTS

✓ People with Parkinson's disease often feel anxious, apprehensive or even depressed about their illness.

✓ Medical attention is needed early in depression.

✓ Confusions and hallucinations may be caused by sensitivity to anti-Parkinsonian drugs, or by other unrelated illnesses.

✓ The combination of Parkinson's disease and dementia makes treatment difficult.

# Disability in Parkinson's disease

If you have just been told that you have Parkinson's disease, I expect you will feel gloomy and despondent. You will have visions of a shuffling, bent old person, see yourself in a wheelchair and feel disheartened by the possibility of your family and friends having to look after your every need. These feelings are common, but in many cases they are unjustified by subsequent events.

## GETTING THINGS IN PERSPECTIVE

It is important to understand the illness and to get it into perspective. Whereas it is true that some patients do end up with severe physical and mental disabilities, many do not. A lot depends on how old you are when the condition is first noticed. If, for instance, you have been fit and reasonably active and when you are, say, 74 you develop a shaking in one hand and a little stiffness and slowness of movement in that arm, we can safely say that your life expectation won't be reduced, and that the Parkinsonian symptoms are unlikely to cause much disability before you are in your eighties; even then, they may not be serious. Other coincidental illnesses—arthritis, bronchitis, heart disease and strokes— are more likely to cause difficulties.

If you are one of those afflicted when unusually young, say in your thirties or forties, the rate of worsening is often slow, and although severe physical problems are eventually likely, you will probably have many years of good function and be able to continue with your work and home life. Moreover, new modifications of treatment develop so quickly, that the outlook may well be much better during the next decade.

## DETERIORATION IS OFTEN SLOW

In general the course of the illness is a slow one. Sudden deterioration is unlikely unless brought about by other illness or by use of the wrong drugs. In my experience and that of others, the disease remains stationary for five, 10, or more years, in as many as perhaps 15 to 20 per cent of patients and disabilities are mild and do not increase during this period. Why this is so, we do not know.

## IS THE TREATMENT WORKING?

The effects of treatment are vitally important in determining how much trouble the illness causes. The effects of treatment are usually most gratifying for several years. In order to assess how effective treatment is, or the stage of the disease at any one time, it is helpful to record the main problems, signs and disabilities. This is done in the consulting room. However, we also have several scales for classifying the stages of the illness. Overall severity is rated on the established, but probably oversimplified, Hoehn and Yahr scale (named after the individuals who developed it).

There are also detailed scales describing problems in walking, feeding, dressing and other Activities of Daily Living (ADL). The lengthy Unified Parkinson's Disease Rating Scale (UPDRS), King's College Hospital Scale, and North Western University Disability Scale, are also in common use.

## HOEHN AND YAHR SCALE FOR RATING SEVERITY OF DISABILITY

**Five stages have been arbitrarily assigned:**

**Stage I** Unilateral disease only

**Stage II** Bilateral mild disease

**Stage III** Bilateral disease with early impairment of postural stability

**Stage IV** Severe disease requiring considerable assistance

**Stage V** Confinement to bed or wheelchair unless aided

Webster is a simpler scale for assessment, and takes only 5 to 10 minutes. It is used by doctors to record slowness of movement (bradykinesia), rigidity, tremor, gait, speech and so on. It comprises 10 items graded 0 to 3 each, producing scores of 0 (no signs of disability) to a maximum of 30 (most severe). There are two additional useful features: a check on balance and the ability to get up

## WEBSTER SCORE FOR PARKINSON'S DISEASE

Each item is graded according to a specific schedule which is scored 0 to 3:

1. Bradykinesia of hands
2. Rigidity
3. Posture
4. Arm swing
5. Gait
6. Tremor
7. Facies
8. Seborrhoea
9. Speech
10. Self-care

**TOTAL:** / 30
**Date:**
**Time:**

[Additional items suggested (scored 0 - 3, 1 point each):

Balance
Rising from chair
Dyskinesia

MENTAL STATE:
(scored 0 to 3)

Confusion
Hallucinosis
Dementia

from a chair. There are also scales for assessing dyskinesia (jerky, twitching movements).

The chart on page 30 may be helpful in assessing your progress periodically and the effects of treatment.

You will see that by repeated use of these scales it is possible to measure the degree of improvement resulting from any form of treatment.

Just as the quality of life has been enhanced by drug treatment, so has the duration of life. Before the levodopa drugs, the life expectancy was about 12 years. Many Parkinsonian patients now have a normal life expectancy and are more likely to succumb to unrelated, common illnesses that affect the elderly.

## KEY POINTS

✓ Not all Parkinson's disease patients end up with severe physical and mental disabilities.

✓ Specially designed scales are used to assess the severity of disability and the impact of treatment.

✓ Many patients now have a normal life expectancy.

# DYSKINESIA SCALES

A. Duration: The time when dyskinesia is present during waking hours:

0 = none
1 = 1 to 25 per cent of waking hours
2 = 26 to 50 per cent
3 = 51 to 75 per cent
4 = 76 to 100 per cent

B. Severity of dyskinesia

0 = noticeable, mild but not disabling
1 = mildly disabling
2 = moderately disabling
3 = severely disabling

**N.B. Additional scales can be made 0 to 3 for painful dyskinesia; and for dystonias**

## DAILY PARKINSONISM MONITORING CHART
### Check with the key below, then please fill in hourly

Name: ...........................................................................................................................................................

|  | 7am | 8am | 9am | 10am | 11am | 12pm | 1pm | 2pm | 3pm | 4pm | 5pm | 6pm | 7pm | 8pm | 9pm | 10pm |
|---|---|---|---|---|---|---|---|---|---|---|---|---|---|---|---|---|
| **Mobility** | 2/e/md | 1 | 1 | 1 | 1 | 2 | 3/md | 2 | 1 | 1 | 2 | 2 | 2/md | 2 | 1 | 1 |
| **Tremor** | + | - | - | - | - | + | ++ | - | - | - | - | ++ | + | - | - | - |
| **Dyskinesia** | - | ++ | - | - | - | + | - | ++ | - | - | - | - | - | + | - | - |

**Mobility Key**
1. Walks unaided
2. Walks with help of one
3. Cannot walk

T. Resting Parkinsonian tremor +/++/+++
D. Dyskinesia +/++/+++

**Drug Key**
ap = apomorphine
art = benzhexol (Artane)
br = bromocriptine (Parlodel)
dis = orphenadrine (Disipal)
e = selegiline (Eldepryl)
ly = lysuride
md = Madopar
sin = Sinemet

# Medical treatment

Treatment is aimed at abolishing as far as possible the symptoms and disabilities caused by the illness. We do not yet have any drugs that will cure the disease or affect the natural progression. What the available drugs will do is to reverse the symptoms by replacing the essential chemicals, such as dopamine, necessary for normal transmission of nerve impulses and control of movements.

## KEY FEATURES OF TREATMENT

●Treatment should be tailormade to suit the needs of each individual, and will need adjustments of fine-tuning at intervals over the entire course of the illness. In Parkinson's disease it is not enough to put the patient on one tablet, three times per day, and leave it at that!

●Treatment should always be governed by symptoms and by disability. For example, at the onset, when symptoms may be mild and inconspicuous, it is often best to give no drugs at all.

●Correct management means more than drugs alone. Active and positive efforts are necessary from you and from relatives. Help is also needed from general practitioners, physiotherapists, occupational therapists and various welfare services at certain times in the disease.

### Who will treat you?

In my view, most patients should be referred to a hospital specialist—usually a neurologist—at an early stage in order to confirm the diagnosis and to obtain advice about the immediate and future prospects of treatment. Patients are seen at intervals to assess their progress and drug treatment. Thereafter, the neurologist will arrange for regular follow-up at intervals which vary from two months to a year.

Increasingly, GP's are continuing treatment for patients, but obviously should refer them to the consultant if problems develop.

## DRUG TREATMENT

I have already described the deficiency of essential dopamine in the brain and the excess of acetylcholine relative to the dopamine, that occurs in Parkinson's disease. Thus, early treatment consists of drugs called anticholinergics, which diminish acetylcholine and restore the balance with dopamine.

Later, amantadine may be introduced; this substance has mild dopamine releasing properties, boosting dopamine levels; it is weakly anticholinergic and has few side-effects.

Some neurologists introduce dopamine agonists (pergolide or bromocriptine) next, because they cause less jerky, twitching movements (dyskinesia) than does the drug most often used for established disease, namely levodopa. However, within the first three to four years, most patients do need a levodopa drug.

Levodopa is converted to active dopamine. The old pure levodopa has now been replaced by combinations of levodopa with carbi-

## ANTICHOLINERGIC DRUGS

| Drug | Trade name | Single dose per tablet or capsule | Dose range per day |
|------|-----------|-----------------------------------|---------------------|
| Orphenadrine | Disipal Biorphen (syrup/elixir) | 50mg 25mg/5ml | 100 to 300 |
| Benzhexol | Artane Broflex (syrup) | 2 or 5mg 5mg/5ml | 6 to 15mg |
| Benztropine | Cogentin | 2mg | 1 to 4mg |
| Procyclidine | Kemadrin Arpicolin (syrup) | 5mg 2.5mg/5ml and 5mg/5ml | 7.5 to 30mg |

dopa (Sinemet) or levodopa with benserazide (Madopar). These drugs are the mainstay of drug treatment and more effective than other drugs currently available. Several drugs are available as syrups and elixirs for patients who have difficulty swallowing tablets or capsules. The striking benefits afforded by these drugs may, in some cases, slowly wear off after five to 10 years, but still offer some relief of symptoms. Patients' needs and responses to therapy vary widely, so do not take too literally the dosages or regimens mentioned here.

If the levodopa drugs are not adequate, another group of drugs, called dopamine agonists, may be used. They stimulate the dopamine receptors rather than supply more dopamine. Pergolide, bromocriptine and lysuride are examples.

Sometimes, apomorphine is used, but this has to be administered by regular injections, rather like a diabetic patient using insulin. It has the great advantage of giving about one hour's (50 to 90 minutes) benefit starting within five to 10 minutes of the injection; this is useful in helping you to handle a pressing social or business engagement.

Selegiline is itself a weak anti-Parkinsonian drug but is valuable in early disease to control symptoms and delay by about one year the use of Madopar or Sinemet. Selegiline also reduces the wearing off of the effects of Madopar and Sinemet which occurs in the later stages of the disease (end-of-dose akinesia).

## Anticholinergic drugs

These are valuable for treating early tremor and rigidity but are not as potent as levodopa in treating slowness, freezing, and falls. They are good at controlling salivation and drooling, since they cause a dry mouth. They work well with levodopa drugs, but are generally tailed off gradually in older patients or if there is any tendency to confusion, hallucinations or memory impairment. Symptoms from an enlarged prostate gland, or any liability to glaucoma may be worsened. Anticholinergic drugs are particularly helpful in drug-induced Parkinsonian states and in the now rare post-encephalitic cases. There is little to choose between the various drugs shown in the table in terms of potency or side-effects.

## Levodopa Drugs

These are the treatment of choice for moderate and severe Parkinson's disease. Rigidity, slowness, posture and often tremor are improved by levodopa drugs. Their good effects may be less marked in the elderly and in those with long-standing illness, because such pati-

## LEVODOPA-DERIVED DRUGS

| Drug | Trade name | Single dose (per tablet or capsule) | Dose of levodopa per day |
|------|-----------|------------------------------------|--------------------------|
| Levodopa with benserazide | Madopar | 62.5/125/250mg | 100 to 800 mg |
| | Madopar CR | 125 | 100 to 1200mg |
| Levodopa with carbidopa | Sinemet | 110/275mg | 100 to 800mg |
| | Sinemet LS | 62.5mg | |
| | Sinemet plus | 125mg | |
| | Half Sinemet CR | 125 | 100 to 1200mg |
| | Sinemet CR | | 100 to 1200mg |

ents may be unable to tolerate a dose large enough to control their symptoms. Levodopa is best given as Sinemet or Madopar.

### Drug dose is gradually increased

Treatment is started with a small dose, taken with food. This is gradually increased until the smallest dose necessary to produce acceptable control of symptoms and disability is reached.

Drugs like Sinemet and Madopar contain a mixture of levodopa and a second drug which concentrates the levodopa in the brain and minimises side-effects elsewhere in the body.

For example, Sinemet 110 contains levodopa 100mg plus carbidopa 10mg; Madopar 250 contains levodopa 200mg plus benserazide 50mg.

### Balancing benefit against side-effects

The best dose is often a compromise between near-total control of all symptoms and side-effects. Many physicians like to keep a little in reserve for future needs. Most patients are untroubled by early side-effects, though occasionally nausea, vomiting or fainting are a nuisance: these are easily overcome by dose adjustments and timing.

### Unwanted side-effects

After one or two years, some patients develop abnormal jerky, twitching (choreic) or writhing (athetoid) movements called drug-induced dyskinesia. They occur one to three hours after a dose when brain levels of dopamine are at their peak. They affect the mouth, tongue, lips and cheeks and often the neck, limbs and trunk. They

## DRUG TREATMENT OF PARKINSON'S DISEASE ACCORDING TO STAGE OF DISEASE

| Symptoms & Disability | Treatment |
|---|---|
| no disability | no drugs or selegiline |
| symptoms a nuisance/ embarrassment | anticholinergics* and/or selegiline |
| stiff and slow despite anticholinergics | add amantadine or pergolide† |
| slow, marked tremor, falls, work in jeopardy | levodopa given as Madopar or Sinemet |
| early dyskinesia or fluctuations | smaller doses often + pergolide† |
| late levodopa failure | long acting Madopar or Sinemet + pergolide, or apomorphine injections |

| | |
|---|---|
| * | not in elderly or confused |
| † | pergolide, bromocriptine and lysuride are alternative, similar drugs |
| Note: | Combinations of drugs are often used |

more often trouble the patient's husband or wife than the patients themselves, for they are embarrassing and unsightly rather than disabling. If severe, they can be reduced or abolished by smaller doses of the drugs, which may then need to be given more frequently. The patients with dyskinesia on Sinemet 275, three times a day, may be relieved of it by Sinemet 110 in five or six doses at intervals of two to three hours. The usual response of Parkinson's disease and other kinds of symptomatic Parkinsonism to levodopa and anticholinergic drugs is shown in the table at the foot of page 36.

### Wearing-off effects

At a later stage of Parkinson's disease the duration of action of drugs seems shorter. You may notice wearing off at the end of each dose (end-of-dose akinesia) before the next tablets are due; or you may be aware of wearing off on waking each morning (early morning akinesia) because the last evening's dose has worn off. Slowness, stiffness, and freezing are the most troublesome features. Sometimes a single dose seems to fail to work often an after-lunch dose. This is sometimes caused by proteins in the stomach and intestine, from the preceding meal, interfering with the absorption of the drug into the bloodstream. Modifying the diet may improve this problem.

The recently developed slow release (controlled-release or CR) preparations are useful in some patients. A single dose in the evening may reduce the troublesome difficulties of turning over in

## SIDE-EFFECTS OF LEVODOPA-DERIVED DRUGS

| | |
|---|---|
| Early in first few days and weeks | Nausea, vomiting, fainting: all wear off within a few weeks |
| Late after 1-3 years | Wearing-off at end-of-dose dyskinesia and dystonia 'On-off' fluctuations Mental confusion, hallucinations |

## RESPONSE TO PARKINSON'S DISEASE AND OTHER KINDS OF SYMPTOMATIC PARKINSONISM TO LEVODOPA AND ANTICHOLINERGIC DRUGS

| Condition | Levodopa | Anticholinergic drugs |
|---|---|---|
| Parkinson's disease | +++ | ++ |
| Drug-induced Parkinsonism | ++ | ++ |
| Multi-system atrophies including progressive supranuclear palsy | +/- | +/- |
| Other causes of Parkinsonism | +/- | +/- |

+++   usually very good
++    moderate
+     some
+/-   variable response

bed, or getting up to the lavatory. It may also control dystonic cramps in the legs and feet, and may give greater mobility on waking, before the first dose of ordinary levodopa is given.

The single dose of a CR preparation at night needs to be used with the usual daytime regimen of ordinary Madopar or Sinemet. An alternative regimen is to take the CR preparation alone, regularly in the daytime, in place of the usual levodopa drugs; the levels of drug in the blood and brain tend to be lower and achieved more slowly. The dose needs to be increased by about 50 per cent above the previous levodopa dosage. This produces a more smooth and even response of symptoms and shorter periods of immobility in the 'off' phase. However, many patients find that they are never fully active or 'on', and prefer the usual shorter-acting Sinemet or Madopar.

### 'On-off' episodes

Later, 'on-off episodes' may develop. The 'on' phase occurs at peak dose and the patient is then mobile and independent, but often has abnormal dyskinetic movements. The 'off' phase consists of sudden freezing, feet sticking to the floor and immobility, sometimes with a feeling of fear and panic. Patients may suddenly switch from 'on' to 'off' and from 'off' to 'on'

"like switching on a light switch". This is disconcerting and may be wrongly thought to be nervous or psychologically caused. Smaller, more frequent doses may ease this difficult problem.

A related problem is painful cramp-like twisting of the ankle and toes that occurs often at the end of the dose—just before the next dose is due, or sometimes at night. This is called drug-induced dystonia.

You will appreciate that all these drug manipulations require patience and skill both from patient and physician. It is often necessary to admit such patients to hospital for specialised care, frequent checks and ratings of symptoms, side-effects and dosage in order to achieve the fine-tuning for optimal performance. This may take one to two weeks.

### Other side-effects

The other important unwanted effects are mental disturbances, such as confusion, disorientation and failing memory and concentration. As you grow older, abnormal movements or mental disturbances may make it necessary to reduce the dosage of levodopa. This may make you much calmer and more contented, but, it is likely to increase your Parkinsonian features— slowness and rigidity, the difficulties in walking, posture and falls. In the end, most families find it easier to handle a patient who is slow, perhaps immobile, but rational than one who is more active, but disorientated and confused.

## DOPAMINE AGONISTS

It is fashionable to introduce these drugs at an early stage, before levodopa, because they cause less dyskinesia than levodopa, and, it is thought that they may delay the appearance of levodopa dyskinesias and fluctuations. Another use is to introduce a dopamine agonist when dyskinesia, mental side effects or 'on-off' fluctuations develop. It is then helpful to add a dopamine agonist, which stimulates or excites the dopamine receptors into greater activity.

Pergolide, bromocriptine and lysuride are similar dopamine agonist drugs. They are started in small doses and slowly increased every week or so until benefit is apparent without undue side-effects. It may take two or three months until the best stable dose is found. If they are added to Sinemet or Madopar, when the benefit begins it may be possible to reduce the levodopa dose by about 25 per cent.

### DOPAMINE AGONISTS

| Drug | Trade name | Single dose | Dose/day |
|------|-----------|-------------|----------|
| Bromocriptine | Parlodel | 1, 2.5, 5, 10mg | 20-100mg |
| Lysuride | Revanil | 200 mcg | 600-5,000mcg |
| Pergolide | Celance | 50, 250, 1000mcg* | 750-4,000mcg |
| Apomorphine | Britaject | 10mg in 2ml ampoule | 3-30mg |

* Note: 1,000 microgrammes (mcg) = 1 milligramme (mg)

### Side-effects
Dopamine agonists are strong drugs, which reduce all the symptoms of Parkinson's disease, but

their side-effects can be prohibitive. They cause more severe psychiatric complications of confusion, delusions and frank aggressive behaviour in a number of patients. These are usually reversible on reducing the dose, but often it is necessary to stop the drug. These psychiatric complications are especially likely in the over 70's and in those with previous confusion or dementia. Dopamine agonists can also aggravate stomach ulcers and arterial disease in the legs. In general they should not be given to older patients, and should always be supervised by a specialist.

### Apomorphine

This is an old drug that has found a new use. It, too, is a dopamine agonist, but it has to be given by a pump or by injections subcutan-

Apomorphine injections can be helpful, giving about one hour's (50 to 90 minutes) almost certain benefit starting within five to 10 minutes of the injection. This is useful if you have an important social or business engagement. The injections can be repeated two or three times each day, under specialist advice. Dyskinesia can result if the dose is too high, and the correct dose for you has to be found by trial and error, always starting with a small dose.

## SELEGILINE (ELDEPRYL)

This is a weak anti-Parkinsonian drug, but it slightly strengthens the effects of levodopa drugs and it may reduce the 'on-off' swings, especially the immobility in the 'off' phase. It is best given early in the illness, and is useful because

## OTHER DRUGS

| Drug | Trade name | Dose | Dose/day |
| --- | --- | --- | --- |
| Amantadine | Symmetrel | 100 | 200mg |
| Selegiline | Eldepryl | 10mg | 5 to 10mg |
| | Eldepryl syrup | 10mg/5ml | |

eously (under the skin) in the lower abdomen or outer thigh, which many patients or relatives can be taught to give. It causes vomiting unless each dose is preceded by Domperidone, a potent anti-vomiting drug taken by mouth.

it controls most of the early symptoms for one to two years.

The early reports that selegiline had a protective effect, slowing down the disease, have sadly proved to be untrue. A single dose of 10 mg each morning is well tolerated, and side-effects are not common.

## DRUG HOLIDAYS

In resistant cases with random 'on-off' swings and poor control of Parkinsonian symptoms, drug holidays have been tried. The aim is that, by withdrawal of drugs, an attempt is made to rest or to reset the dopamine receptors that have been overdriven by levodopa and other drugs, and to rid the brain of theoretical toxic by-products of these drugs. This is all unproven speculation, and in practice, benefits only sufferers who are plainly overdosed.

Restabilisation is then necessary, in hospital with hourly recording charts of Parkinsonian signs, disability, mental performance and side-effects. These observations usually reveal the problem, and then we often stop inessential or weak acting drugs and those medications thought to be unnecessary for coincidental ailments. The dose of levodopa is reduced by 50 to 75 per cent and as side-effects disappear, drugs are reintroduced gradually until the smallest effective dose is found. Simplification is the hallmark of effective treatment.

In difficult cases, it is sometimes helpful to apply an apomorphine or levodopa test dose. A single high dose is given after a 24 hour period of drug withdrawal, and the effects give a good indication of whether or not the dopamine receptors are still responsive. If they are not, there is plainly no sense in persisting with dopaminergic drugs. The test gives important information that predicts future responses to treatment. A single dose of 250 mg Madopar or an injection of 2 to 10 mg apomorphine will demonstrate dopamine responsiveness by showing improvement of at least 20 per cent in one of the standard rating scales I discussed earlier.

## SOME DRUG WARNINGS

Certain drugs should not be used in Parkinson's disease. I have mentioned the major phenothiazine tranquillisers and anti-psychotic drugs (neuroleptics). These drugs may also be suggested for nausea or for dizzy attacks but should seldom be used in Parkinson's disease. Monoamine-oxidase inhibitors used for depression are not allowed, but tricyclic antidepressants are in order. Patients with certain types of glaucoma or skin melanoma should not take levodopa drugs.

Vitamin B6 (pyridoxine), present in multi-vitamin capsules and medicines, and used for pre-menstrual tension, blocks the action of levodopa, but there is no interaction if given with Sinemet or Madopar. If in doubt, you should always consult your doctor.

## KEY POINTS

✓ Drug treatment reverses the symptoms of Parkinson's disease by replacing the essential chemicals necessary for normal transmission of nerve impulses and control of movements.

✓ Drugs are chosen to match the stage of the disease and need adjustments at intervals over the entire course of the illness.

✓ Pure levodopa has been replaced by combinations of levodopa with carbidopa (Sinemet) or levodopa with benserazide (Madopar). These are the most effective drugs currently available.

✓ Unwanted side-effects can be reduced or abolished by altering the drug dose.

✓ When wearing-off effects of drugs are troublesome, the recently developed slow-release (controlled release or CR) preparations are useful in a few patients.

✓ Dopamine agonists should not be given to older patients and should always be supervised by a specialist.

# Surgery for Parkinson's disease

This consists of either destruction of tiny parts of the brain (stereotactic surgery) or transplantation of dopamine-producing tissue into the brain.

## STEREOTACTIC SURGERY

Surgical treatment for Parkinson's disease is rarely recommended. Thirty years ago there was a vogue for placing tiny destructive lesions in the basal ganglia by means of a stereotactic apparatus which permitted very accurate placement of the lesion. This was fairly effective in controlling tremor and rigidity—if it was one-sided. Stereotactic surgery is of no benefit in correcting the facial expression, weak voice, slowness of movement, stooped posture and tendency to fall. Indeed, sometimes these symptoms are made worse.

Stereotactic surgery is still used, especially in Japan for early one-sided tremor and rigidity, if they fail to respond to other measures. In most specialised centres in the UK and the USA, however, it is seldom used because levodopa drugs, despite their shortcomings, have, in general, proved so effective. Occasional patients may benefit from such operations if their main problem is one-sided shaking and rigidity uncontrollable by drug treatment. The decision requires expert neurological advice.

## NIGRAL TRANSPLANTS

In 1981 in Sweden, the first attempts were made to transplant the patient's own adrenal medulla (autografts) into the caudate nucleus, a part of the basal ganglia involved in the transmission of dopamine. The adrenal medulla is rich in amines, including dopamine. The hope was that this would provide an added source of natural dopamine. Results in early patients were disappointingly slight and any doubtful benefit wore off quickly. This work did, however, show that the surgery was possible, that the adrenal tissue took on its new blood supply and to some extent formed new nerve connections in the receptor site.

More publicity was given to the extension of this work in younger patients in Mexico. Two of the 12 patients treated died within six months, but from unrelated causes. Benefit was claimed for rigidity, akinesia and tremor, but improvement was variable and was delayed from three to 10 months and in some cases for more than a year. This was not a controlled trial and the florid publicity in the national press caused more than a little sceptical criticism amongst neuroscientists in the USA. Isolated reports of similar procedures in North America have confirmed the soundness of this cautious reception. Subsequent operations transplanting the adrenal medulla have shown variable and slight benefits, with increasing periods of activity and less akinetic 'off' periods in each 24 hours. This surgery affords no predictable reduction of anti-Parkinsonian drugs and the morbidity after operation is considerable. For the moment this approach has been abandoned.

## TRANSPLANTATION OF FETAL TISSUE

Other methods have been attempted, notably the transplantation of substantia nigra from human fetuses. This area is the main site of loss of dopamine stores in human Parkinson's disease, so it makes good sense to replace it with the same tissue.

The number of such operations performed is still very small, largely because it involves major surgery, there are ethical problems in using fetal donor tissue, and the long-term benefits are not yet proved. Strictly controlled studies, comparing operated against non-operated cases of similar age, sex and severity of illness are essential before we can say that the operation is valuable in certain types or stages of the disease, or conversely, of no benefit to any patient.

## THE NEED FOR CAUTIOUS OPTIMISM

For the present, these techniques are exciting, but must be viewed with cautious optimism. It is not known whether transplantation alters the progression or outcome of Parkinsons's disease. It is not known whether any such benefit will be lasting. And it is not known whether those agent(s) that primarily cause the disease will also destroy the graft. We must also remember that Parkinson's disease reflects a disorder not only of dopamine, but of many other neurotransmitters which may not be replaced by the grafts, even if the grafts work. These techniques hold out promise, but must be scientifically tested. Meanwhile, no patient should feel deprived of an implant until we have far more information.

## KEY POINTS

✓ Stereotactic surgery can occasionally be beneficial for one-sided shaking and rigidity uncontrollable by drug treatment.

✓ Attempts to transplant dopamine-rich fetal tissue into the brains of patients with Parkinson's disease need to be repeated under strictly controlled conditions before the value of such surgery can be judged.

# General management

Drug treatment is the most important single measure in reversing the symptoms and disabilities of Parkinson's disease, but there is far more to the treatment of the patient than the administration of drugs alone. Many of the problems faced by patients are not caused by Parkinson's disease itself, but by the coincidental accompanying conditions from which many people suffer and which may need separate medical attention. Some patients are diabetic, some have high blood pressure, some asthma, some heart disease or bronchitis, and many have arthritis. Thus the care of the whole patient is an essential approach from your doctor—GP or specialist.

## IDENTIFYING THE PROBLEMS

Certain problems occur commonly in Parkinson's disease and the first step is to identify them. Then, we must outline means of helping to correct them. Here are some common problems in movement you may have noticed, and there are many more:

- walking slowly
- walking with short, shuffling steps
- walking through doorways causing you to stop or hesitate
- freezing of feet to the floor
- turning in a narrow space without falling
- swinging the arms automatically when walking
- getting out of a chair
- standing straight instead of hunched forwards
- turning over in bed
- getting on and off a toilet
- using the hands with fine manipulations, dressing and undressing
- writing smaller, shaky and spidery

- using screwdrivers
- sewing on buttons or crocheting

## PHYSIOTHERAPY

Physiotherapy has specific benefits for specific problems; it also has a generally beneficial effect in boosting morale, in persuading the patient that something active is being done, and that he or she is playing an active part in the treatment. The motivation, personality and the attitude of both patient and therapist have a marked influence on the general benefits obtained. Bad habits are better eradicated early than late. In advanced illness motivation may be poor, memory and concentration impaired and effective cooperation may be impossible.

Assessment is the first step. This includes:

- the physical disabilities
- learning capacity and mental state
- home circumstances
  the availability of able bodied friends and family to continue to practice any instructions.

### Exercises

Exercises and activity are important, as they mobilise joints and muscles, lessen stiffness and improve posture. They aim to:

- correct abnormal gait
- correct bad posture
- prevent or minimise stiffness and contractures of the joints
- improve use and facilities of the limbs
- provide a regimen which can be used at home by the patient.

The physiotherapist will teach you how to sit straight in a high, upright chair, aided by a cushion in the back.

Pull your heels in under the front edge of your chair and throw your weight forward to get up more easily.

Regular exercise is beneficial whenever disabilities permit. It helps to maintain your muscle tone and strength and helps to prevent contractures and stiffening. Walking is one of the most valuable exercises. Most people in the early stages can walk a mile or two each day, sometimes much more. A conscious effort should be made to keep the back straight, shoulders back, head upright and to take slow, long strides. Even more severe cases can often walk 300 or 400 yards, and perhaps repeat this once or twice every day. Slippery surfaces, snow, ice and wet leaves should obviously be avoided.

The physiotherapist will concentrate on teaching you to sit straight, often in a high upright chair, aided by a cushion in the back. She or he will show you how to concentrate on striking the heel down when walking, how to improve moving from sitting to standing, by pulling your heels in under the front edge of the chair and throwing the weight forward as you get up. Standing in front of a long mirror may help you to see and correct any stoop or bent posture of the neck and trunk.

## OCCUPATIONAL THERAPY

A wide range of home aids is available, many of which should be available on the NHS, though some may need to be purchased priva-

tely. A home visit by an occupational therapist is invaluable, and he or she will usually prepare a report for the hospital consultant describing specific problems, the need for gadgets, hand rails, high seats and other provisions. Wide handles on cutlery, anti-slip kitchen surfaces, lever arms on taps, raised working surfaces in the kitchen and greenhouse, Velcro fasteners to garments and shoes, are examples of the ways in which you can make easier your activities and independence.

### Keep at it

Constant repetition and practice are necessary at home, especially when the therapist is no longer badgering you; there is no substitute for 'do it yourself'! Exercises may be made easier and more rhythmical if performed to music on a cassette, CD or radio. Visits to out-patient therapy may be helpful and encouragement may be obtained by group exercises. Therapeutic Holidays, including vigorous activity, can sometimes be arranged (see *Useful Addresses* on page 59).

### Appliances

As the disease progresses, some patients require aids to activity. Walking sticks add to your stability and are socially unobtrusive. A tripod held in one hand does the same thing on a wider base. Zim-

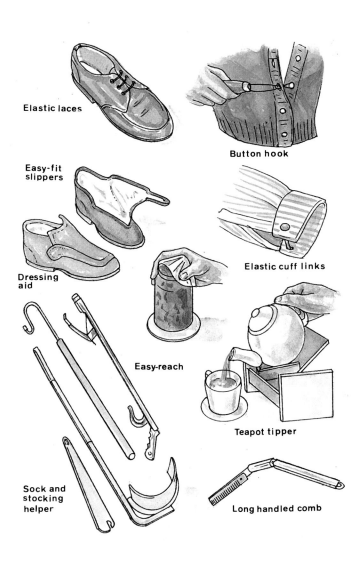

Elastic laces

Button hook

Easy-fit slippers

Dressing aid

Elastic cuff links

Easy-reach

Teapot tipper

Sock and stocking helper

Long handled comb

Household gadgets can help.

mer frames are not recommended except as a short-term measure when mobilising after injury or operation in hospital. They break the natural thythm of walking. If, however, they are fitted with wheels, they are valuable. Delta frames with two 'legs' and a front wheel or a rolator with two legs and two wheels are helpful. Brakes add to your sense of security.

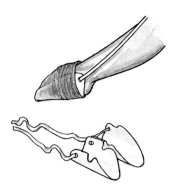

Stocking helper

Aids to activity can help to provide a sense of security.

Individual exercises are aimed to help balance, lengthen your stride and perhaps relieve the pain of a frozen shoulder—a common complication. Manual dexterity may be improved by practice with blocks, jigsaws and certain games. Grab rails fitted near your bed, in the lavatory and bathroom are helpful. Buttons and zips can be replaced by Velcro fasteners. Casual or elastic sided shoes or trainers may be much easier than lace-up shoes.

Large-handled knives, forks and spoons, stick-on plates and egg cups can save spills. Many of these can be supplied or recommended by the physiotherapist or occupational therapist. The Welfare Department of the Parkinson's Disease Society is also able to advise.

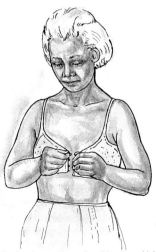

Getting dressed is easier with a bra which fastens at the front.

It is of enormous advantage if there is good liaison between the hospital based physiotherapist, occupational therapist, the social worker and the ward team. They will meet to discuss plans and joint assessments when patients are admitted to the ward, and will continue supervision, where possible, after you go home. They will also link up with the GP and district welfare services.

lack of variation in pitch and volume of the voice. Assessment by a speech therapist will examine the way you breathe, move your lips, tongue and jaw in the formation of speech—all elements that we do unconsciously or automatically.

In Parkinsons's disease, the voice box (larynx) is deficient and produces a monotonous pitch, lack

Communication aids can help with speech therapy.

## SPEECH THERAPY

Many patients are embarrassed and frustrated by their speech. You may find that you speak quietly, are unable to shout and that friends are always asking you to repeat yourself, or to speak up, please. Speech may be slurred and hesitant with

of volume control and lack of stress of certain sounds. Your voice may sound hoarse, quiet and monotonous. Speech therapy may use audio feedback in which you hear your own speech after a measured latent interval; this can modify and improve the voice and speech output. This and other manoeuvres can, to a modest extent, help to retrain the voice and speech, but dramatic improvements are not common.

## Aids to communication

Communication aids include' Edu-Com Scanning', a device to point to a word or picture showing your intention and meaning. 'Microwriter' links a TV, printer or speech synthesizer and can be of occasional help to patients when speech training is unsuccessful. The use of a personal computer (PC) may help you to write letters and perform business activities and attend to your finances from home. Modern programmes are fairly easy to learn if you are a newcomer to this technological world, and there is a wide range of recreational games and educational material that may occupy and expand your interests.

## DIET

Patients with Parkinson's disease require no special diets but should have a balanced enjoyable diet with fresh meat, fish, fruit and vegetables, like everyone else. Sometimes, a dose of Madopar or Sinemet does not work, particularly with an after-lunch dose. This may occur because proteins in the stomach and intestine, from the preceding meal can interfere with the absorption of the drug into the bloodstream. Your specialist may advise you to have a low-protein lunch with small amounts of meat,

fish, poultry, eggs or cheese, but to include these foods in the main evening meal, after which you may not wish to be as active as during the day.

## SOME GENERAL OBSERVATIONS

With the help of your GP you should obtain up-to-date medical support and supervision of your drug and physical treatment, and advice about any possible side-effects. More specialised guidance is available from consultants in clinics who should supervise most patients—where staffing levels and facilities permit. The welfare services and hospital units also provide support from physiotherapists, occupational therapists and social workers when the need arises, but currently, the provision and quality of support is variable.

Activity throughout the illness is the keynote. Do as much as you can, but be sensible and don't overdo it, to the point of exhaustion. Three walks of 400 yards each are at least as beneficial as one of 1200 yards. You will also have to make certain adjustments to you lifestyle, but these are usually obvious, and changes are gradual so you have plenty of time to make these alterations. You may have to allow a little longer to get dressed or go to work, or to plan and pack for holidays or journeys. It may take two goes to mow the lawn instead of one. Try not to let this irritate you; a little planning, allowing more time, will make most tasks possible.

Don't get fanatical about crackpot schemes you read about, or about gossip you hear. A lot of money can be wasted on charlatan remedies, health foods, acupuncture, osteopathy and so forth. Medical opinion has no rooted objections to these therapies, but does not use them unless they have been carefully and scientifically tested, so that it is clear if they are of benefit or not.

## CONCLUSIONS

Although there has been considerable progress in the last few years, Parkinson's disease remains something of an enigma. We know that there is degeneration of certain small but vital areas of the brain, but it is not just a condition caused by ageing. Its effects are complex, but the main one is a lack of an essential chemical transmitter, dopamine, which can be effectively replaced by modern drug treatment. This permits a full and active life for many years.

The Parkinson's Disease Society and other organisations fund medical and social research on a large scale. As a result, there is hardly a year goes by without some important addition to knowledge, additions that are of practical importance to each and every sufferer from the disease.

All new discoveries require careful scientific scrutiny before they can be accepted as valid. There are many avenues of progress under investigation.

Although we are dealing with a slowly progressing illness in most cases, you should remember that most patients have a normal lifespan, which includes many years of activity and enjoyment. Sufferers from Parkinson's disease can face the future with measured optimism.

# Questions & Answers

●What causes Parkinson's disease?
We don't know the cause. Investigations have sought environmental factors such as contaminants of food, water and air, and exposure to poisonous chemicals at work, but have failed to produce an answer. Although there is a weak hereditary factor, it is not the cause, but may make certain people more susceptible to unidentified substances, to which we may be exposed.

●I have been under a lot of stress. Could that be the cause?
No. Stress and tension may cause a temporary worsening of symptoms, but they do not cause the disease. Depression is a common problem in Parkinson's disease and may reduce your general efficiency, drive and ability to cope. It is generally much improved by antidepressant drugs.

●Will I pass it on to my children or grandchildren?
Although there is a slightly higher incidence of perhaps one in 20 cases in close relatives, Parkinson's disease is not an inherited disease.

●I have heard that Eldepryl (selegiline) will slow down the disease. Should I take it?
Trials in the USA have now shown that selegiline does not affect the disease process in the brain and has no effect in reducing the rate of progression. It is, nonetheless, useful early in the illness and acts by relieving early symptoms, thereby delaying the time when it is necessary to start levodopa drugs. Side-effects are infrequent and mild.

●Is there any advantage in delaying the start of levodopa drugs?
Because the benefit of levodopa

drugs tends to fade after five to 10 years, it is generally thought sensible not to start them too soon, i.e. before symptoms are of more than nuisance value, and are beginning to interfere with work and leisure. There is no advantage in delaying once this time is reached, and the benefits are usually obvious and will improve your quality of life.

● What will be the effects of levodopa, and will it have side-effects?
Within a month of so, stiffness, slowness of movements, walking difficulties and posture start to improve. Shaking does not always disappear, but may be reduced. Benefit continues to increase as the fine tuning of dose and timing are carefully monitored. A few patients have sickness or faintness in the first few weeks, but taking tablets on a full stomach, and starting with small doses that are increased slowly will allow them to cope with this. Abnormal movements, fluctuations in effects—before and after each dose, and mental problems can develop later in the illness, but adjustments of drugs and dosage often or abolish these symptoms.

● I have taken Madopar (dopamine) for two years. Why am I now getting these funny twitching movements?

These are probably dyskinesias or dystonias caused by a slight overspill or excess of drug on the sensitive receptors in the brain. They usually occur some 30 to 60 minutes after each dose, and last for a few minutes. Your doctor may advise a slight reduction in dose, given at shorter intervals. A controlled release (CR) preparation helps some patients.

● Why is it taking so long for the tablets to work, and why do they wear off so quickly?
After a few years the body does not absorb or distribute levodopa as efficiently, and the dopamine receptors do not respond quite so effectively, as at the start of treatment. Alteration by your physician of the dose and frequency often overcomes this problem.

● I find that I can't concentrate or remember things like I used to. Is Parkinson's disease responsible?
Memory and concentration often diminish with normal ageing, irrespective of Parkinson's disease. If you have become depressed, this can also affect concentration and memory, and often improves with simplification of, or additional, drug therapy. Only a small percentage of Parkinson's disease sufferers become demented.

● Am I likely to benefit from a transplant?

Adrenal transplants are now thought to be largely ineffective. Fetal transplants are, for the time being, in the experimental stage. They have been shown to be feasible, but their value is not yet established.

Meanwhile, no patient should feel deprived of an implant until we have far more information.

# Useful Addresses

## Parkinson's Disease Society

36 Portland Place, London W1N 3DG
Telephone: (0171) 383 3513.

## Citizen's Advice Bureau

For local information and up-to-date addresses. see your local telephone directory.

## Disabled Living Foundation

Visits by appointment only for advice about equipment and appliances.
380-384 Harrow Road, London W9 2HU
Telephone: (0171) 289 6111.

## Publications

*Help for Handicapped People.* A DHSS booklet available from the Parkinson's Disease Society or your local social security office.

*Coping with Disablement.* Published by the Consumers' Association,
14 Buckingham Street,
London WC2N 6DS.

*Holidays for the Physically Handicapped* from the Central Council for the Disabled,
34 Eccleston Square,
London SW1V 1PE.

# Index